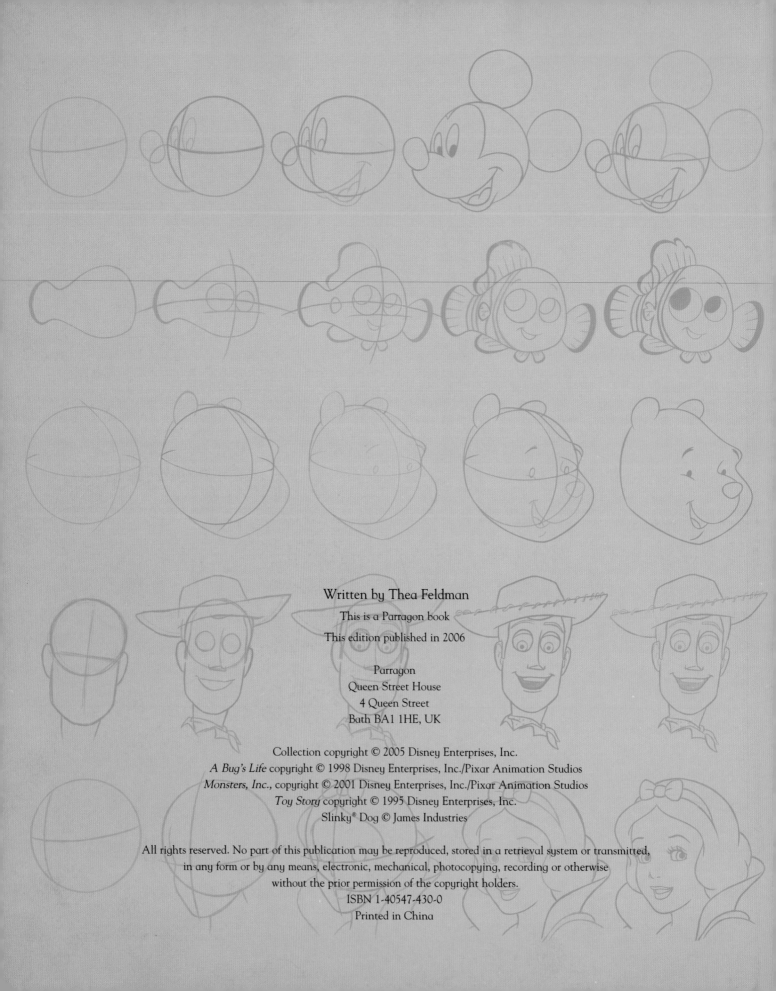

Written by Thea Feldman

This is a Parragon book
This edition published in 2006

Parragon
Queen Street House
4 Queen Street
Bath BA1 1HE, UK

ISBN 1-40547-430-0
Printed in China

CONTENTS

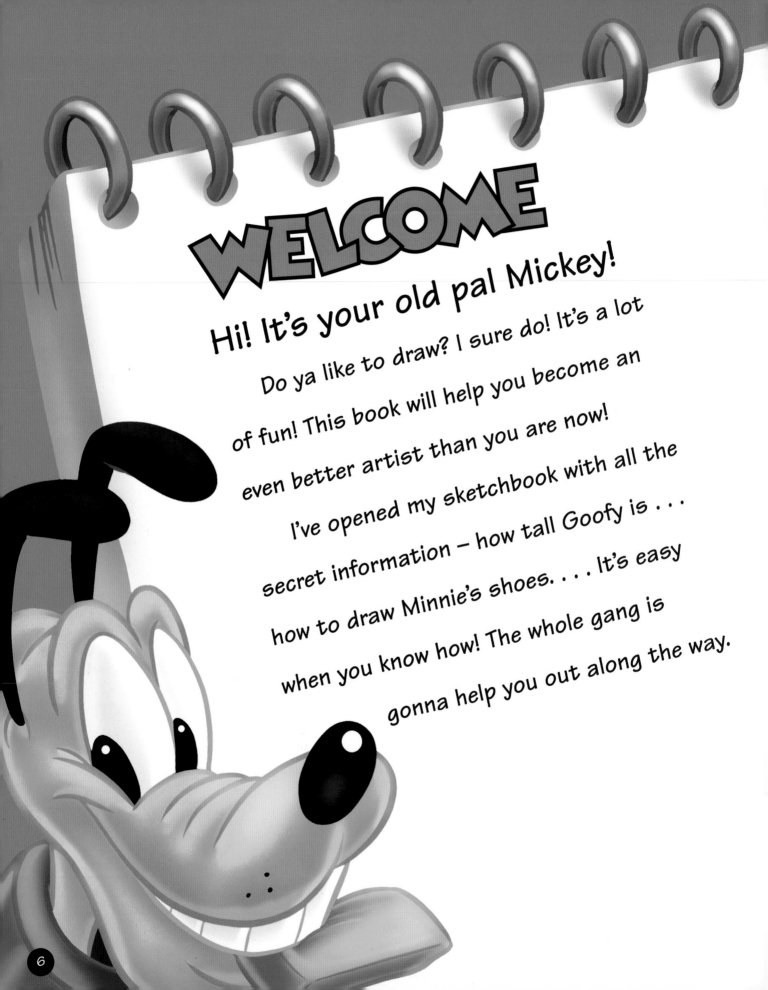

WELCOME

Hi! It's your old pal Mickey!

Do ya like to draw? I sure do! It's a lot of fun! This book will help you become an even better artist than you are now!

I've opened my sketchbook with all the secret information — how tall Goofy is . . . how to draw Minnie's shoes. . . . It's easy when you know how! The whole gang is gonna help you out along the way.

Before you begin, gather up these swell supplies:

- some pencils
- paper – a sketch pad is best, but any plain paper will do
- pencil sharpener
- eraser

C'MON! LET'S GET STARTED!

Later on, when you colour your drawings, you may want to try out some felt-tip markers, crayons, coloured pencils, watercolours, or even acrylic paint.

BASICS

Before learning to draw the characters, it's a good idea to get warmed up. Start by drawing simple shapes like circles and ovals. Don't worry about making them perfect; just keep your wrist nice and loose. When you feel comfortable with your shapes, move on to the steps.

1

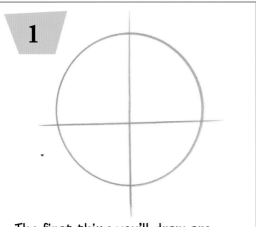

The first thing you'll draw are guidelines to help position the features of the character.

Usually artists draw characters in several steps. Sometimes the steps are different, depending on what you're drawing. The important thing to remember is to start simply and add details later. The blue lines show each new step, and the black lines show what you've already drawn.

2

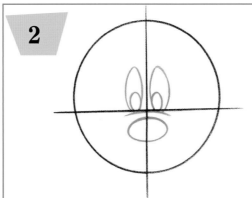

Next you'll start to add details to your drawing. It will take several steps to add all the details.

3

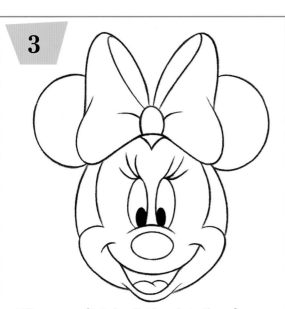

When you finish all the details of your drawing, you can go back and erase your guidelines. You can also darken your lines with a pen or marker.

Goofy's learned all the steps, and now he's ready to paint the finished drawing!

THE GANG

Before we get started, let's get to know Mickey and his friends.

MICKEY MOUSE

Mickey Mouse is always friendly and outgoing. Everybody likes him.

MINNIE MOUSE

Minnie Mouse is Mickey Mouse's sweetheart and friend.

DONALD DUCK

Donald Duck has quite a temper, but he's still lots of fun to be around.

Check out how big (or small) the characters are compared to one another. When you draw them together, you'll want to make sure that you don't make Donald taller than Goofy! Remember that everyone is just about the same height except Goofy, who's the tallest.

DAISY DUCK

Daisy Duck is Donald's favourite gal. She's quite fashionable.

GOOFY

Goofy is a pretty silly guy. Make sure you draw him having lots of fun.

PLUTO

Pluto's one happy pup! His best pal is Mickey Mouse, who also happens to be his owner.

MICKEY MOUSE

Drawing Mickey's Face

STEP 1

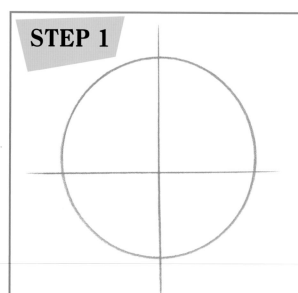

Start with a circle. Add centre lines to help position Mickey's features.

STEP 2

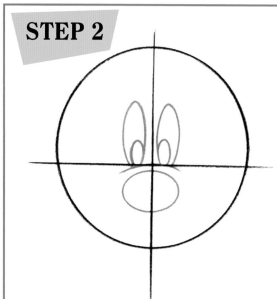

Now add Mickey's eyes and nose. His eyes rest on the edge of one centre line. Add a little curve right below his eyes.

STEP 3

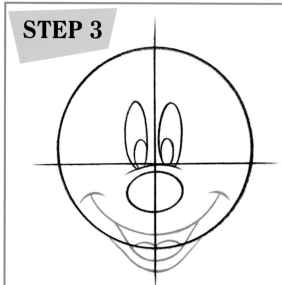

Add Mickey's smile and chin. The top portion of his mouth follows the same curve as his nose. See how his chin extends below the circle of his head.

Pluto is Mickey's favourite pup, and Mickey is Pluto's best pal.

STEP 4

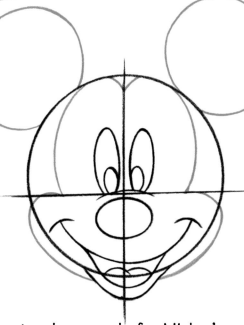

Draw two large ovals for Mickey's ears. Add curved lines to form the area around his cheeks and eyes. (This is called the "mask".)

STEP 5

Erase your guidelines and clean up the drawing.

STEP 6

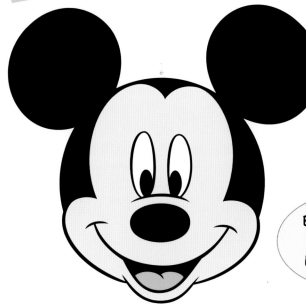

Now colour your drawing of Mickey.

BE SURE TO MAKE HIM HANDSOME!

MICKEY MOUSE
Drawing Mickey's Head

STEP 1

Start with a circle. Add centre lines to help position Mickey's features.

STEP 2

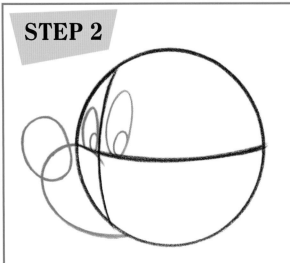

Add Mickey's eyes and nose. His eyes rest on the edge of one centre line. For his nose, draw a curved line for the snout. Position the bulb of his nose on the end.

STEP 3

Add Mickey's smile and chin. The top of his smile follows the curve of his nose. See how his chin extends below the circle of his head.

Mickey's eyebrows can show how he's feeling.

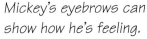

STEP 4

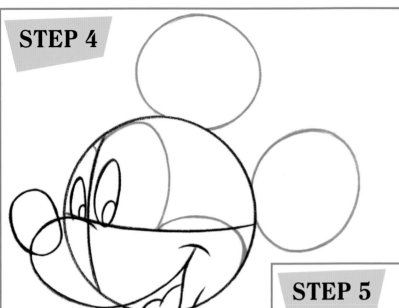

Draw two large ovals for Mickey's ears. In this view, one of Mickey's ears is on the top of his head, and the other is on the back. Add curved lines to form the mask.

You can always see both of Mickey's ears, no matter which direction his head is turned.

STEP 5

Erase your guidelines and clean up the drawing.

STEP 6

Now colour your drawing of Mickey.

When Mickey is surprised, his ears go up.

MICKEY MOUSE
Drawing Mickey's Body

When drawing the characters' bodies, notice the curved line going from top to bottom in Step 1. This line is called the line of action. The line of action is a guideline to give your character direction and movement.

STEP 1

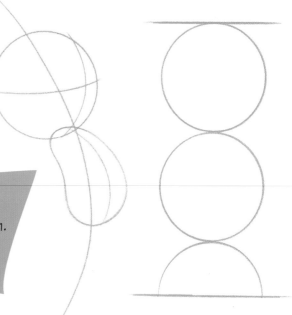

Start with a circle. Add a pear shape for Mickey's body. Mickey's height is $2\frac{1}{2}$ times the size of his head.

STEP 2

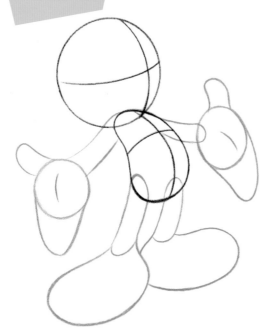

Add Mickey's arms, legs, hands, and feet.

When the tops of Mickey's hands show, be sure to add the stitching lines to his gloves!

STEP 3

Add Mickey's ears, pants, and shoes.

STEP 4

Fill in all the details for Mickey's head that you learned.
Don't forget to add his tail!

STEP 5

Erase your guidelines and clean up the drawing.

STEP 6

Now colour your drawing of Mickey.

Mickey's shoes are slightly longer than his hands.

MINNIE MOUSE

Drawing Minnie's Face

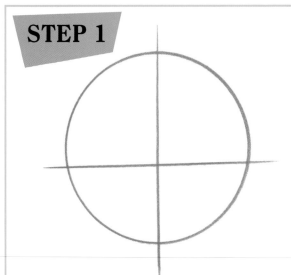

Start with a circle. Add centre lines to help position Minnie's features, just as you did for Mickey.

STEP 2

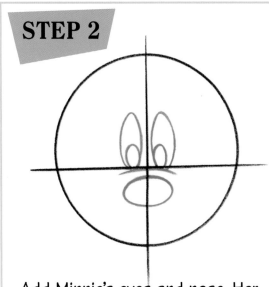

Add Minnie's eyes and nose. Her eyes rest on the edge of one centre line.

STEP 3

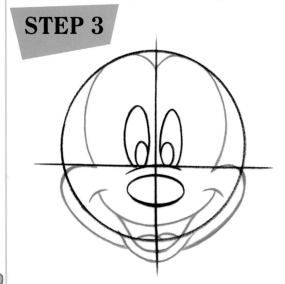

Add Minnie's smile and chin. The top portion of her mouth follows the same curve as her nose. See how her chin extends below the circle of her head. Add curved lines to form the mask.

Minnie and Daisy are the very best of friends.

18

STEP 4

Draw two large ovals for Minnie's ears and a great big bow on top of her head. Don't forget her eyelashes!

Don't forget Minnie's eyelashes. The middle lashes are longer than the others.

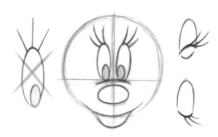

STEP 5

Erase your guidelines and clean up the drawing.

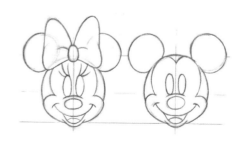

Minnie's and Mickey's heads are similar, but Minnie's eyes are slightly larger and wider than Mickey's. Her open mouth is slightly smaller than his.

STEP 6

Now colour your drawing of Minnie.

DONALD DUCK

Drawing Donald's Face

STEP 1

Start with a circle. Add centre lines to help position the features.

STEP 2

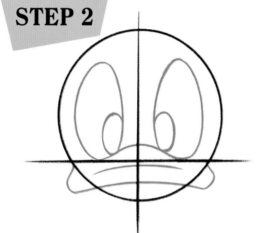

Add Donald's eyes and the top of his bill. His eyes rest on the edge of one centre line. Draw the curved lines for his bill.

STEP 3

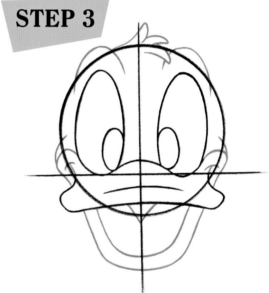

Add Donald's eyebrows and tufts on the top of his head. See how his lower bill curves below his head. His cheeks are very curvy when he smiles. Now add a little triangle for his tongue.

Goofy's silly attitude sometimes irritates the hot-tempered Donald, but Mickey usually manages to keep the peace.

STEP 4

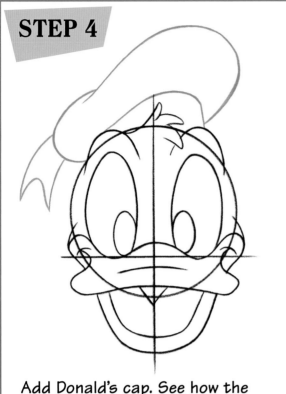

Add Donald's cap. See how the hatband and the ribbon are the same width.

STEP 5

Erase your guidelines and clean up the drawing.

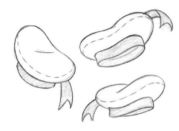

Donald's hat is soft and flexible but always holds its shape.

STEP 6

Now colour your drawing of Donald.

GAWRSH! THAT'S A FUNNY HAT!

DONALD DUCK
Drawing Donald's Body

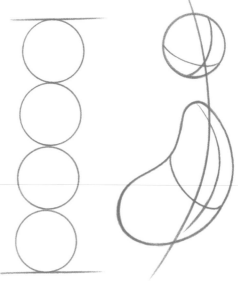

Start with a circle. Add a jelly bean shape for Donald's body. Donald's height is about 4 times the size of his head.

STEP 2

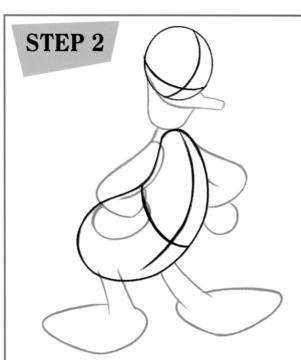

Add Donald's arms, legs, hands, feet, and bill.

Donald's hands are almost as long as the height of his head.

STEP 3

Sketch in Donald's clothes.

22

STEP 4

Draw Donald's face as you learned on pages 20 and 21. Add the details of his clothes. Don't forget his tail!

STEP 5

Erase your guidelines and clean up the drawing.

STEP 6

Now colour your drawing of Donald.

DAISY DUCK
Drawing Daisy's Face

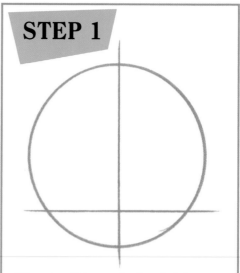

Start with a circle. Add cross lines to help position Daisy's features.

STEP 2

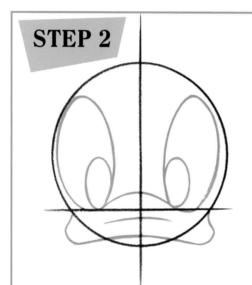

Add Daisy's eyes and the top of her bill. Notice how her eyes are rounder and more angled than Donald's. The bottoms of her eyes and the top of her bill fit together smoothly.

STEP 3

Add Daisy's eyebrows and the lower part of her bill. Now add the little triangle for her tongue, just as you did for Donald.

Daisy is just crazy for Donald.

STEP 4

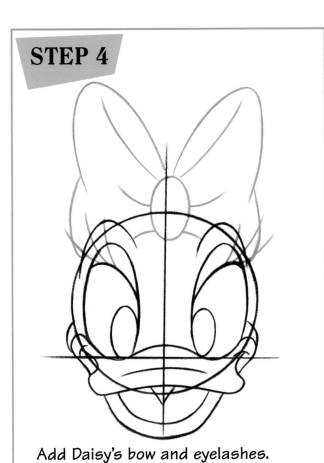

Add Daisy's bow and eyelashes.
She has three eyelashes over each
eye. The middle lashes are longer
than the others.

STEP 5

Erase your guidelines and
clean up the drawing.

STEP 6

Now colour your drawing of Daisy.

BETTER
SHARPEN YOUR
PENCIL FOR DAISY'S
EYELASHES!

GOOFY
Drawing Goofy's Face

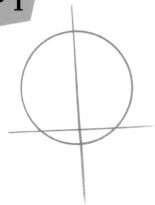

Start with a circle. Then add cross lines as shown to help position Goofy's features. In this expression, part of Goofy's face is on an angle, so you'll make the centre lines angled, too.

STEP 2

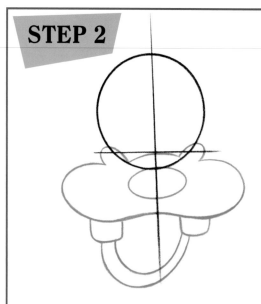

Add a squished oval beneath the circle for Goofy's nose. Then add his cheeks, teeth, and mouth.

STEP 3

Add Goofy's big oval eyes and tongue.

Goofy's head is similar to Pluto's.

STEP 4

Add Goofy's hat and ears. His ears are like big teardrops.

STEP 5

Erase your guidelines and clean up the drawing.

STEP 6

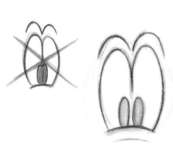

Notice how the whites of Goofy's eyes touch each other. Just make sure you keep his pupils separate.

Now colour your drawing of Goofy.

Goofy's hat is about 1 head long. It's squishy-looking and leans to one side.

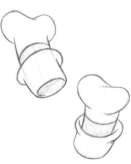

PLUTO
Drawing Pluto's Head

Start with a circle. Add centre lines to help position Pluto's features. The circle for Pluto's head is much smaller than for the other characters.

STEP 2

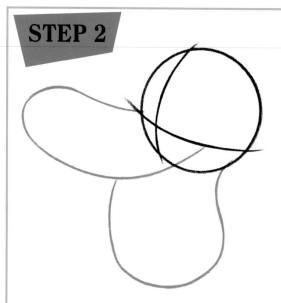

Sketch in the snout and lower jaw. Pluto has a long nose pointing forward and a long, rounded jaw dropping down from the circle of his head.

STEP 3

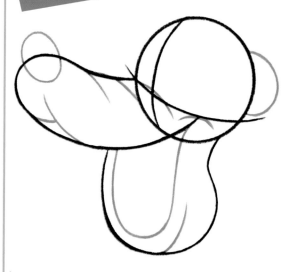

Add the details of Pluto's nose and mouth. Don't forget to add the knob on the back of his head.

Together, Mickey and Pluto have lots of fun.

STEP 4

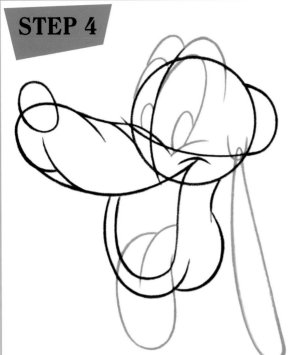

Add Pluto's eyes, eyebrows, and tongue. Pluto's eyes are long ovals, and his tongue hangs down from his mouth. Now add his ear.

STEP 5

Erase your guidelines and clean up the drawing.

STEP 6

Now colour your drawing of Pluto.

ENOUGH, ALREADY! LET'S GO BACK TO PAGE 20!

PLUTO
Drawing Pluto's Body

STEP 1

Start with a circle. Add a pear shape for Pluto's body. Pluto's height is about $4\frac{1}{2}$ times the size of his head.

STEP 2

Sketch in Pluto's legs and head.

STEP 3

Start to add Pluto's face and ears. Sketch in his collar and add some detail to his feet for his toes.

Pluto has three pads on the bottom of each paw.

His three toes are stubby.

STEP 4

Fill in all the details for Pluto's head that you learned on pages 28 and 29. Don't forget to add his tail.

Pluto's ears can act together to accentuate a mood or an expressive pose.

STEP 5

Erase your guidelines and clean up the drawing.

His collar hangs loosely at the back of his neck.

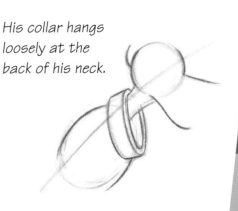

STEP 6

Now colour your drawing of Pluto.

How to Draw
PRINCESSES

Disney princesses can be found in a fairy-tale castle, an enchanted wood, a French countryside, a desert kingdom – even under the sea! Although their stories may be similar – overcoming problems to reach "happily ever after" – each princess brings something special to her tale. Over the years, that "something special" has changed, but the beauty and love that shine in each princess have always remained the same.

Written by
Catherine McCafferty

How to Use This Chapter

Are you ready? Let's start by drawing Cinderella's head. Just follow these simple steps, and you'll be amazed at how fun and simple drawing can be!

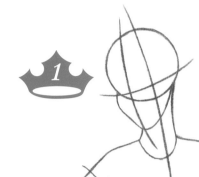

Step 1
Start your drawings in the middle of your paper so you don't run out of room.

Step 2
Each new step appears in blue, so draw all the blue lines you see.

Step 3
Refine the lines of your drawing. Then add the details.

coloured pencils

Step 4
Darken the lines you want to keep and erase the rest.

Step 5
Use markers, coloured pencils, crayons, or paint to add beautiful colours.

Snow White

Snow White is a beautiful young princess who is badly mistreated by her wicked stepmother, the Queen. When creating Snow White, Walt Disney decided to make his first feature princess look more like a pretty "girl next door" than like a glamorous princess. Snow White does have rose-red lips, ebony hair, and skin as white as snow that win her the title of "fairest one of all". But her rounded face and figure also show her youth and innocence.

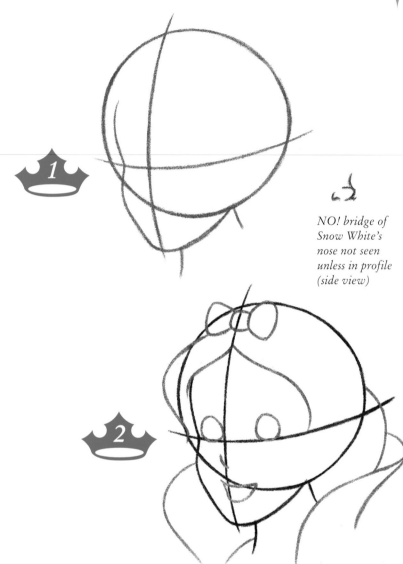

NO! bridge of Snow White's nose not seen unless in profile (side view)

Snow White's hair is drawn with soft curves

eyelashes curl out from her eyelids

top lip is thinner than bottom lip

lips are soft and not too full

Snow White's
features follow
these guidelines

Snow White

Even when she's abandoned in the forest, Snow White's kindness shines through and wins her the friendship of all the forest animals – as well as the love and loyalty of all of the Seven Dwarfs. When you draw Snow White, be sure to show the soft, sweeping lines in her dress and the gentle arm movements that emphasize her cheerful, sweet disposition and her joy for life.

Snow White's hands are rounded and soft like this . . .

. . . not sharp and pointed like this

draw the legs as a guide, even though they're covered by skirt

YES! skirt is wider than hips

NO! skirt is too close to hips

feet are small and delicate

Snow White
is about 6
heads tall

lines are graceful, with
no sharp angles

NO! not angular

figure is
rounded

NO! not
too curvy

Cinderella

Cinderella's story seems much like Snow White's at first: Cinderella is treated badly by her stepfamily, but she overcomes all to win the love of a prince. She is also as pretty as can be, whether she appears as a simple house maiden with her hair pulled back or as a glamorous ball guest with her hair swept up. Still, Cinderella is a very different kind of princess than Snow White is. Whereas Snow White wishes and waits for her love to appear, Cinderella wills her dreams to come true, and she goes to find her Prince Charming at the ball.

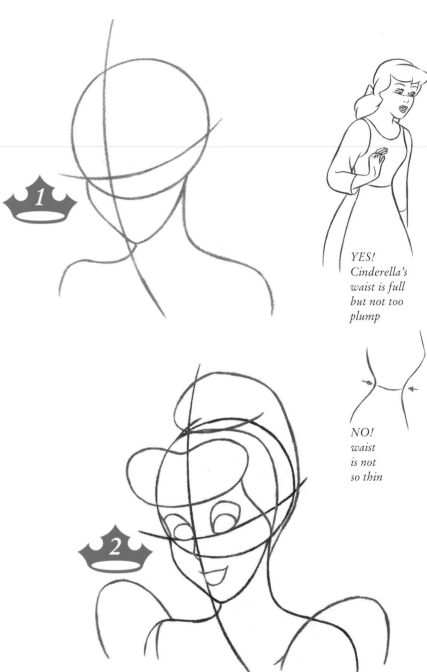

YES! Cinderella's waist is full but not too plump

NO! waist is not so thin

Cinderella has almond-shaped eyes

YES! eyelids have slight S-curve

NO! not droopy – avoid sad eyes

YES! just slight
suggestion of nose

NO! nose is not a
full shape

YES! head-
band curves
only a little

NO! too round

headband is
straighter on top
than on side

Cinderella

Cinderella's beauty and graceful movements are evident as she runs down the stairs in her simple, homemade gown, but they are even more obvious at the ball. When she first arrives in her gorgeous dress (thanks to her Fairy Godmother), she immediately attracts everyone's attention, including Prince Charming's. When you draw her sweeping gown with billowing curves, show just a bit of the elegant lace underneath.

Cinderella's fingers are long and slender

YES! angles are soft and smooth

NO! angles are not sharp

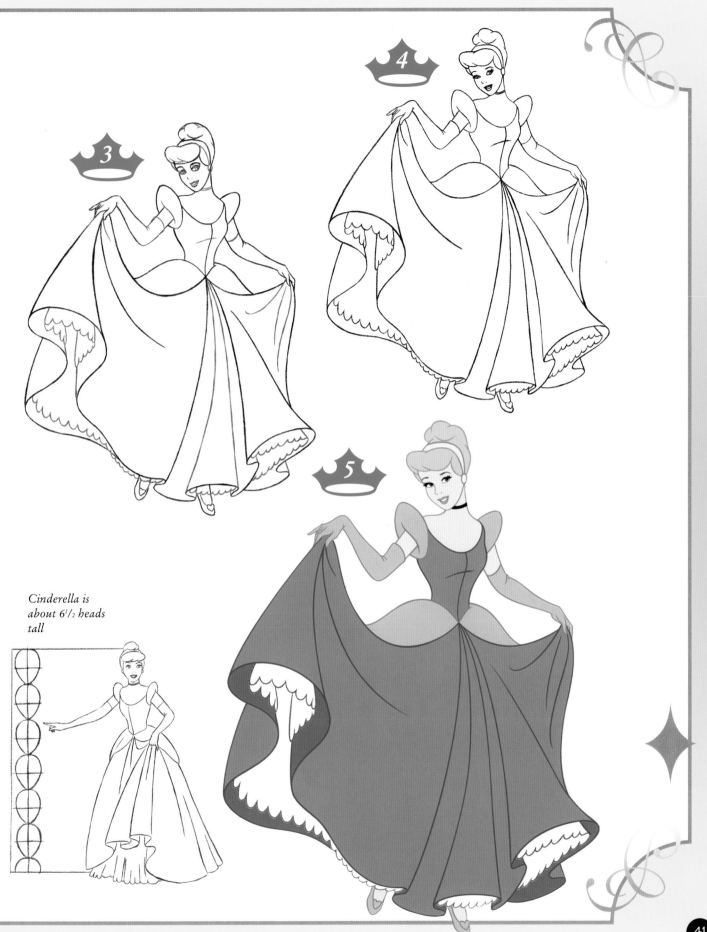

Cinderella is
about 6½ heads
tall

Sleeping Beauty

Though 16-year-old Princess Aurora has been gifted with beauty, she looks very different from both Snow White and Cinderella. She appears older - more like a woman than like a young girl. Princess Aurora spends the early years of her life in the forest as the "peasant" Briar Rose, where she wears a simple dress and holds back her wavy, waist-length hair with a headband. This is how she looks when she first meets Prince Phillip.

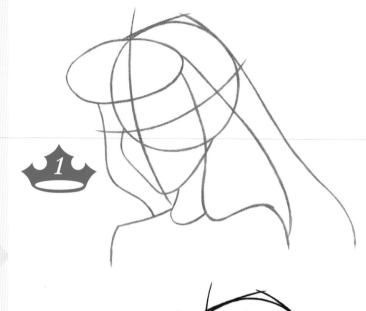

1

YES! Sleeping Beauty's hair extends behind head at an angle

NO! not straight down the back of head

2

eyes tilt up slightly

YES! eyes end in pointed corners and have one thick eyelash

NO! not round – don't draw individual lashes

top of head is
fairly flat

point here

Sleeping Beauty's
features are more
angular than
Snow White's or
Cinderella's

Sleeping Beauty

When Aurora is awakened from her sleep by a kiss from Prince Phillip, she is saved from the curse placed upon her at birth – and she gets to marry her true love! Now when she dances with her prince in the palace, her simple dress is exchanged for a lovely gown, and a beautiful tiara replaces her plain headband. Use long, slightly curved lines for her skirt to show how regal this princess has become.

Sleeping Beauty's hair curls like this at the back

when she dances, hair swings out like this

3

4

5

Sleeping Beauty is about 6¹/₂ heads tall

waist is very slim

large fringe on left

big curl on right

YES! curls are closed, like this

NO! not open curls

Ariel

1

YES! Ariel's fringe puffs out over her forehead

NO! hair doesn't cover face

In many ways, *The Little Mermaid's* Ariel starts out as a very different character from Snow White, Cinderella, or Aurora. She is a confident, headstrong, and passionate teenager who knows exactly what she wants – and will do anything to get it. In fact, she is a princess among princesses, with no fewer than six royal sisters! Ariel lives with her sisters and her father, King Triton, under the sea in Atlantica. And her wavy red hair – a new hair colour for a Disney princess – flows with the currents in her underwater kingdom.

2

YES! Ariel's eyes are wedge-shaped

NO! not triangular . . .

. . . nor round

YES! lips are smooth curves

NO! there's no "dimple" on top lip

hair billows out, especially underwater

each eyebrow is
one thin line

YES! thin
eyebrows

NO! not thick

YES! oval nose is
angled like this

NO! not horizontal
like this

Ariel

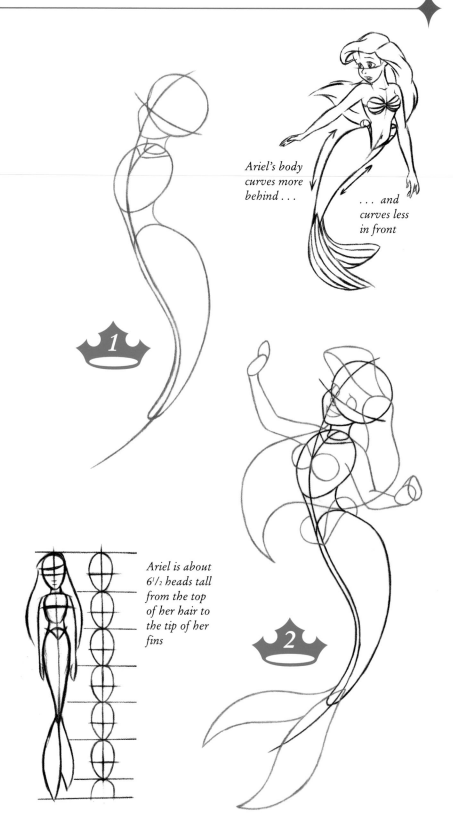

Ariel's body curves more behind . . .

. . . and curves less in front

Ariel probably changes the most of any of the princesses – physically, at least. To get her prince, she trades her voice for legs and feet so she can live on the land. But even without speaking, she's able to win the heart of Prince Eric. Try drawing her as we first meet her, wearing her seashell mermaid outfit and swimming freely under the sea.

Ariel is about 6$\frac{1}{2}$ heads tall from the top of her hair to the tip of her fins

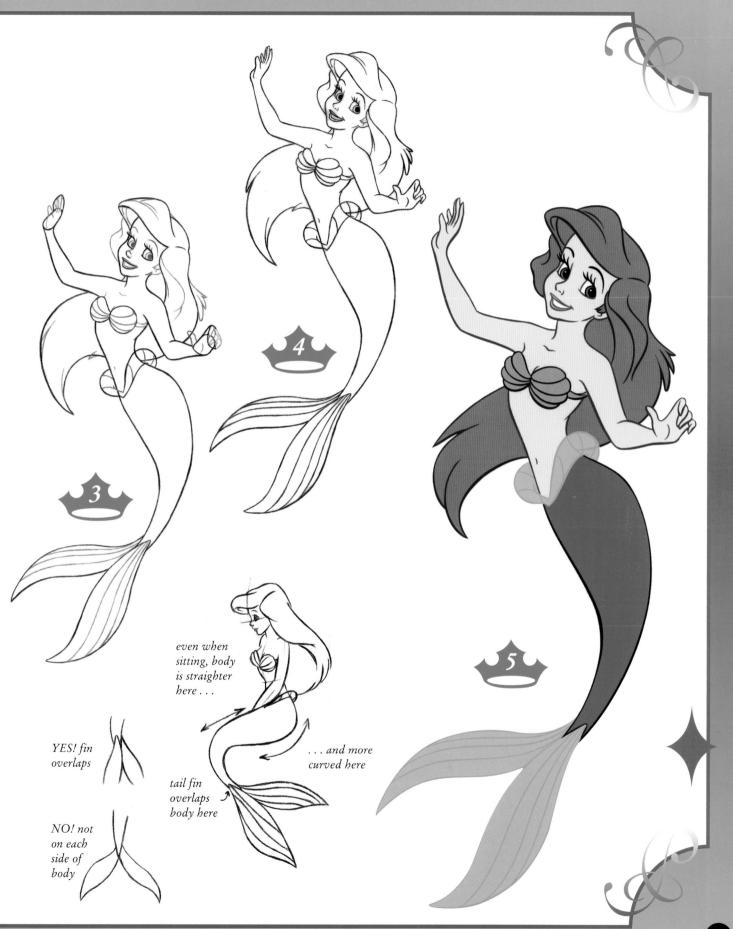

even when sitting, body is straighter here . . .

. . . and more curved here

tail fin overlaps body here

YES! fin overlaps

NO! not on each side of body

Belle

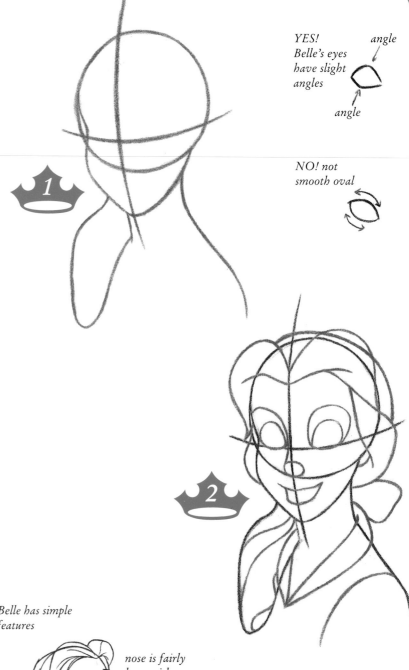

Beauty and the Beast's Belle may like to read and daydream about princes and princesses, but she doesn't live the life of royalty. And she certainly isn't looking for a prince – especially if the closest thing to a "prince" in her town is the conceited Gaston! Down-to-earth Belle keeps her brown hair pulled back in a simple ponytail as she leads a "normal life" in her small, provincial town. Her large, almond-shaped eyes capture the sense of wonder and excitement she feels about new ideas and new places.

YES! Belle's eyes have slight angles

angle

angle

NO! not smooth oval

Belle has simple features

nose is fairly long with defined bridge

thin upper lip

YES! upper lip is thinner than lower lip

NO! not even sizes

YES! eyebrows
are smooth
and thin

NO! not thick
or angular

Belle's facial features
follow these guidelines

1

2/3

1/3

0

hair bow extends
beyond chin line

4

3

when eyes close, angle
of eyes is less dramatic

5

Belle

Belle's prince is horrifying at first – a handsome man trapped in the body of a hideous-looking beast. But Belle soon warms up to his gentle nature, and when she prepares to join the Beast for dinner, she dresses in a beautiful ball-gown and wears a hairstyle befitting a princess. Draw Belle in her elegant, yellow gown, ready to waltz with the Beast in the grand ballroom.

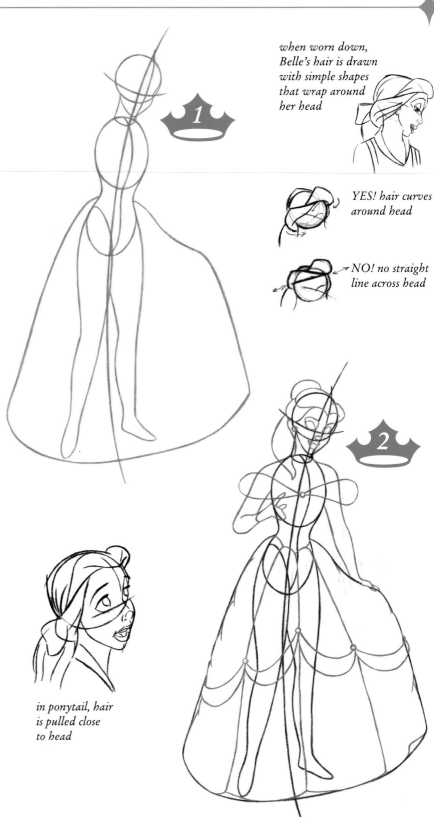

when worn down, Belle's hair is drawn with simple shapes that wrap around her head

YES! hair curves around head

NO! no straight line across head

in ponytail, hair is pulled close to head

Belle is about
6¹/₂ heads tall

Jasmine

Like Aurora, *Aladdin's* Jasmine is about to have her fateful 16th birthday at the beginning of her story. But while Aurora's fairy "aunts" keep hopeful princes away, Jasmine's father hopes that his daughter will marry one of the many princes who come to see her. But Jasmine has other ideas. She would rather marry for love – and she chooses the handsome, young street thief, Aladdin. Jasmine's dramatic features emphasize her exotic beauty, making her unique among the Disney princesses.

Jasmine has almond-shaped eyes

top of eye has flatter curve

bottom of eye has rounder curve

Jasmine's eyes have gentle slant, like cat's eyes

YES! eyes follow bottom of guide-line circle

NO! not straight across face

eyes are about 1 eye-width apart

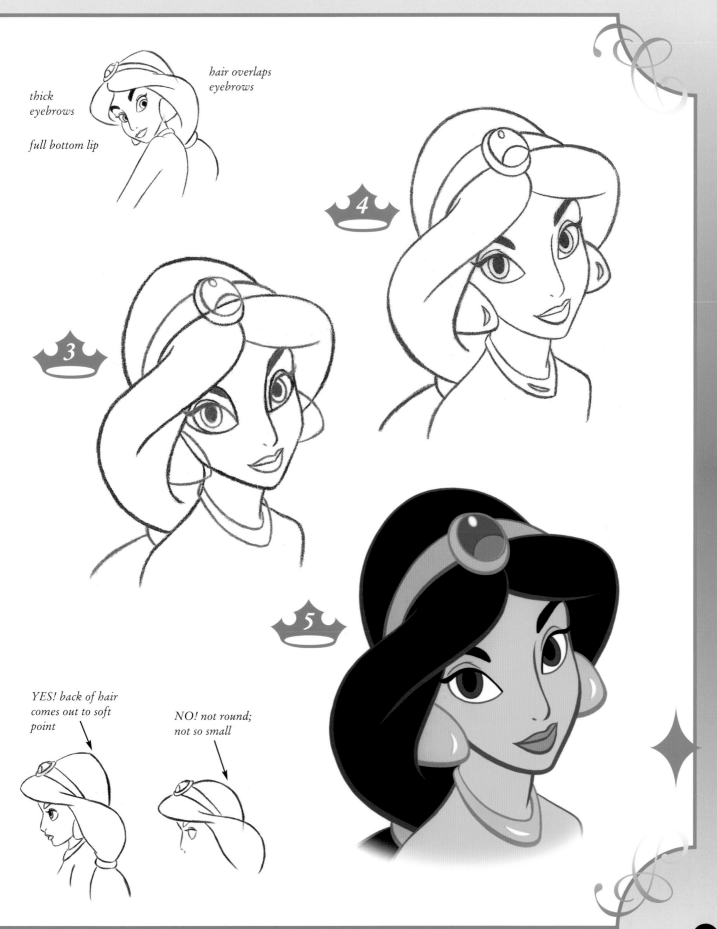

thick eyebrows

hair overlaps eyebrows

full bottom lip

YES! back of hair comes out to soft point

NO! not round; not so small

Jasmine

Jasmine's arms are slender and graceful

elbows fall at waist line

Jasmine's outfit gives her the freedom and flexibility to move quickly – whether she is running away from Aladdin (posing as Prince Ali) or from the evil Jafar. But she looks just as graceful as the other princesses do in their fancy ball-gowns, and every bit a princess. Be sure to draw the sparkling jewel in her headband and the curled toes of her delicate slippers.

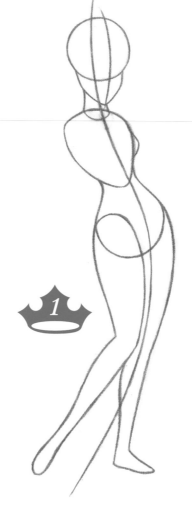

1

2

YES! head-band curves around head like this

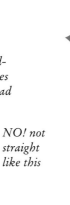

NO! not straight like this

Jasmine is just a little more than 5 heads tall

Tinker Bell

Tinker Bell is both a loyal friend and an overprotective fairy when it comes to Peter Pan. And she has an impish presence all her own. Wherever she goes, a trail of pixie dust follows, and her voice sounds like the tinkling of tiny bells. Tinker Bell's pixie look is carried through in her hair style: Her fringe hangs low on her forehead, and she wears a little bun on top of her head.

YES! Tinker Bell's eyes are slightly tilted but still have rounded shape

NO! not narrow ovals; no pointed corners

YES! flat on top

NO! not round

fringe is a little puffy

mouth is low on face

Tinker Bell has a very upturned nose

Tinker Bell

Because we can't understand what Tinker Bell is saying when she is with Peter and the others, the expressions on her face and her body language are important: They tell you when she is happy, angry, and even jealous. Her tiny costume adds to her pixie look and helps her fly about freely. But don't forget to draw her wings – she couldn't fly without them!

Tinker Bell is about 4 ¹/₂ heads tall

1

2

body is heavier on bottom than on top

YES! legs curve out at thighs and calves

NO! legs don't taper from thick to thin

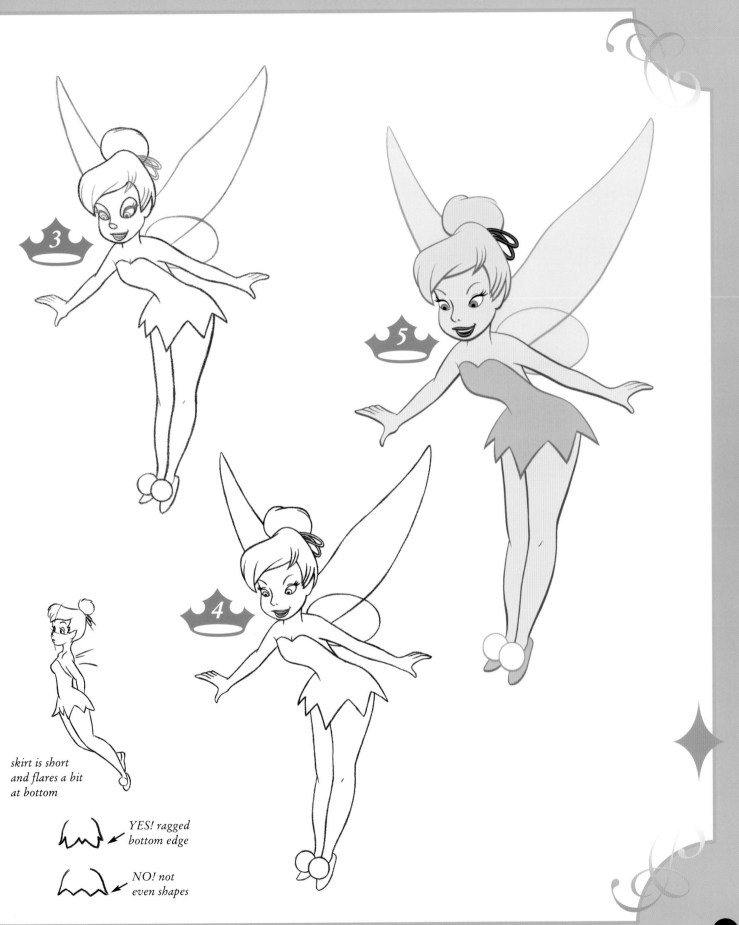

skirt is short
and flares a bit
at bottom

*YES! ragged
bottom edge*

*NO! not
even shapes*

WELCOME TO THE WORLD OF THE HUNDRED-ACRE WOOD

If you look carefully, you might find your favourite bear, **Winnie the Pooh**, playing happily outside his home or thinking in his special "Thotful Spot."

You may also spot **Rabbit** in his garden and **Kanga** out watching her son, **Roo**, playing.

Piglet, Pooh's very small and very timid friend, might be sweeping his house or collecting haycorns to make his favourite haycorn pie.

Christopher Robin's house is safely perched at the top of a hill (a good thing to know in case of a flood—or if you're in need of an extra pot of honey).

And wise old **Owl** can sometimes be spotted flying overhead.

Of course, you mustn't forget **Eeyore** (although he might expect you to).

The gloomy fellow can often be found outside eating thistles or trying to repair his stick house.

If you do happen to see him, give him an extra pat or a hug. (He could use some cheering up!)

Now, if you're ready to learn how to draw all these friendly characters, just turn the page, and we'll begin!

How Tall Is Pooh?

Winnie the Pooh

Piglet

Christopher Robin

Owl

Rabbit

Take a close look at how the characters compare to one another.
Some are tall; some are short; some are just about the same height.
It's important to remember this when you draw characters together -
you wouldn't want Piglet to look taller than Pooh!

Gopher

Eeyore

Tigger

Kanga and Roo

Winnie the Pooh

Drawing Pooh's Face

Pooh is a bear of little brain and big tummy. He has a one-food mind when it comes to honey. But he is also a good friend to Piglet and a perfect pal for "doing nothing" with Christopher Robin. Pooh has a simple sweetness to him that goes beyond the honey stuck to his paws!

How do you draw Pooh's ears?

Too pointy!

Too round!

Pooh's nose is a soft triangle.

Just right!

Sometimes Disney artists look in the mirror to see how to draw certain expressions. If Pooh were drawing a picture of himself, he'd have a perfect model for a giggling bear!

Draw a circle. Then draw two lines crossed in the middle of the circle.

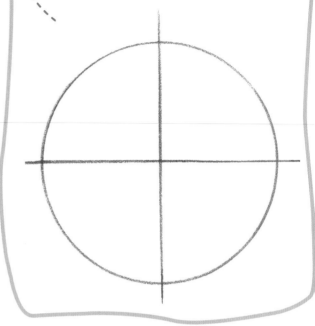

Step 4

Now add his smile.

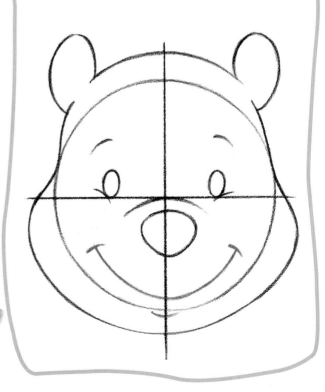

Step 2

Add Pooh's ears, eyes, and chin.
Don't forget his eyebrows!

Step 3

Use the crossed lines to help
you figure out where to draw
Pooh's nose.

Step 5

Carefully erase the guidelines
and clean up the drawing.

Step 6

Now colour your picture!

Winnie the Pooh

Drawing Pooh's Head

With his nose held high and his eyes shut, you won't find a prouder bear.

proud

Notice that Pooh's eyebrows are pushed up and his mouth is O-shaped to show a shocked reaction.

surprised

Drawing one eye shut and pulling up the corners of his mouth puts Pooh into deep thought.

vexed

Step 1

Draw your circle. This time, the crossed lines in the middle are curved.

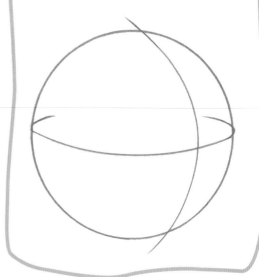

Step 4

Add his nose and mouth. Adding small lines under his eyes shows he's smiling.

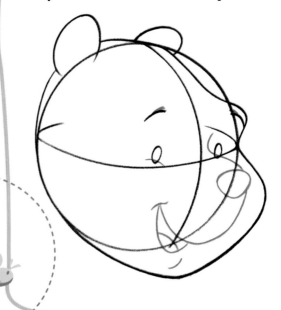

Step 2

Add two small ears, a bump for the brow, and a large cheek.

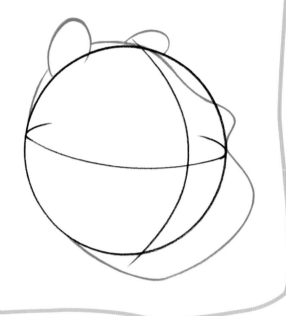

Step 3

Use the crossed lines as a guide when you add Pooh's eyes. Add short, curved lines for his eyebrows.

Step 5

Carefully erase the construction lines and clean up the drawing.

Step 6

Now colour your picture!

Winnie the Pooh

Drawing Pooh's Body

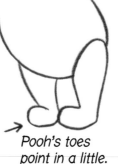

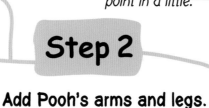

Pooh's toes point in a little.

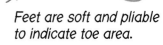

Keep ears apart in profile.

Shirt is loose fitting.

Feet are soft and pliable to indicate toe area.

Step 1

Draw a circle for the head. Then add a pear shape below it for his body.

Step 2

Add Pooh's arms and legs.

Step 3

Use the blue lines to figure out where to put Pooh's eyes, nose, mouth, and shirt.

Piglet thinks the silly old bear is a wonderful friend.

Pooh is about 2 ¹/₂ heads high.

Pooh can have a little thumb if he needs to grab something.

Pooh's arms are almost the same length as his legs.

Step 4

Add sleeves and a collar to Pooh's shirt.

Step 5

You can erase the extra lines when you finish your picture.

Step 6

Now colour your drawing!

Tigger

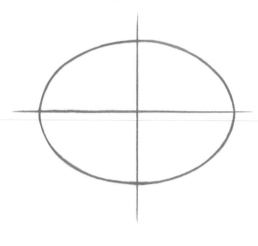

Drawing Tigger's Face

Tigger surely is one of a kind in the Hundred-Acre Wood. He's a good bouncing buddy for little Roo, but his springy style bowls over the others. Tigger is always sure of "what tiggers do best," even before he does something. But perhaps the really "wonderful thing" about Tigger is the bounce he brings to everyone around him.

Step 1

Use the crossed lines to help figure out where to draw Tigger's ears.

Tigger's ears are triangles about as wide as his nose.

When Tigger smiles, his eyes are single lines.

Step 4

Use curved lines to add Tigger's stripes and whiskers.

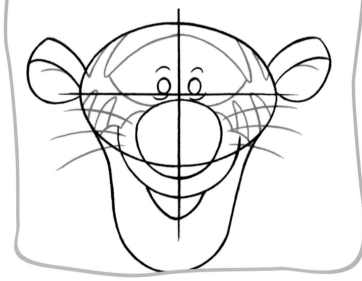

Being a very small animal, Piglet isn't always able to jump as high as his friend Tigger.

Step 2

Tigger's ears point up and out. Don't forget to draw Tigger's big chin.

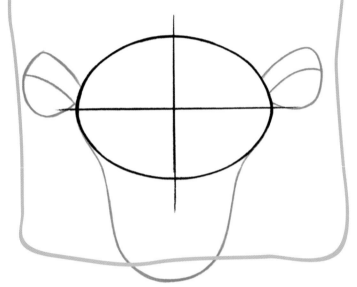

Step 3

Add Tigger's eyes and large nose. Then draw his big grin!

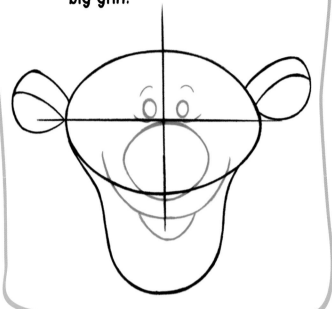

Step 5

Erase your guidelines and clean up the drawing.

Step 6

Colour your picture of Tigger!

Tigger

Drawing Tigger's Head

Step 1

When you draw a sideways view of Tigger, his head is an oval.

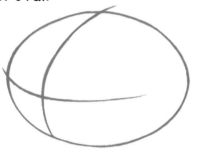

Step 2

Add the ears, chin and neck.

Step 5

Erase your guidelines and clean up the drawing.

Step 6

Colour your picture of Tigger!

When Tigger is sad, his eyebrows go up in the middle, and his whiskers go down.

When angry, his eyebrows go down in the middle.

Step 3

Now draw Tigger's nose, eyes and eyebrows.

Step 4

Use curved lines and triangles to add Tigger's stripes and whiskers.

Gopher (who whistles when he talks) s-s-specializes in s-s-self portraits-s-s – just like Tigger!

Tigger

Drawing Tigger's Body

Tigger's body is a long oval with a short oval on top.

The stripe pattern on Tigger's body varies. Use a mixture of large and small stripes.

Tigger's arms are much longer than his legs.

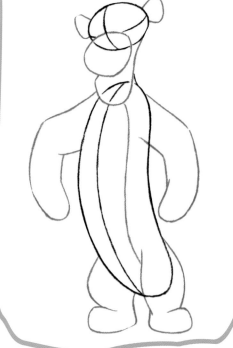

His tail squishes when he bounces.

Step 4

Erase the construction lines and clean up the drawing.

Tigger's body is shaped like a banana.

Step 5

Colour your picture!

Poor Eeyore always seems to be losing his tail. He can't even imagine what it must be like to have a springy tail like Tigger's that never falls off, even with the bounciest of bounces.

Piglet

Drawing Piglet's Head

Piglet is a very small animal. He is little enough to be swept away by a leaf and timid enough to be scared by Pooh's stories of "jagulars." His eyebrows and mouth usually show how he's feeling.

Piglet's head is peanut-shaped.

Make sure his ears don't point toward each other or he'll appear to have horns.

Being a small and timid animal, Piglet is often comforted by the strong and wise Christopher Robin.

78

Step 1

Draw your circle, then the crossed lines.

Step 4

Add floppy ears and a chubby cheek.

Step 2

Draw Piglet's long face with a point at the bottom.

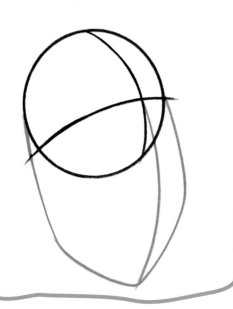

Step 3

Add Piglet's eyes, nose, and mouth along the crossed lines.

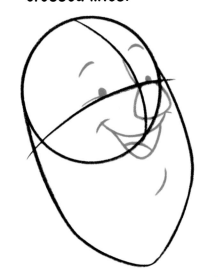

Step 5

Erase the construction lines and clean up the drawing.

Step 6

Now colour the picture!

Piglet

Drawing Piglet's Body

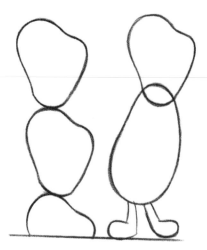

Piglet is 2 ½ heads tall without ears.

His arm and hand can wrap around objects to grab them.

The head is a circle and the body is shaped like a jelly bean.

Add the floppy ears, chubby cheek, and body stripes.

Carefully erase the construction lines and clean up the drawing.

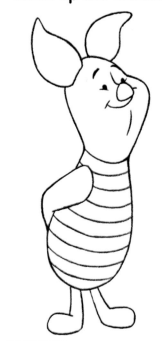

Step 2

Draw the neck and feet.

Step 3

Add the eyes, nose, and mouth along the crossed lines.

Step 6

Now colour your drawing!

Roo and Piglet have something in common: They're both quite small. In fact, Roo happens to fit perfectly inside Kanga's pouch.

Eyore

Drawing Eyore's Head

Things are always looking down for Eyore. With a tail that comes loose and a house that falls down, he's always ready for things to go wrong. Still, Eyore manages to smile once in a while, even though he's almost always gloomy.

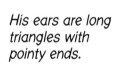

His ears are long triangles with pointy ends.

His mane falls forwards.

Piglet, being a very small animal, is easily frightened.

Step 1

Draw a circle with crossed lines for the head.

Step 4

Little curved lines around Eyore's eyes make him look sad.

Step 2

Then add a shape like a sack for his nose.

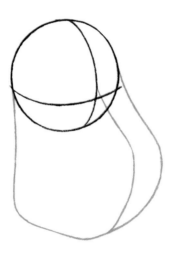

Step 3

Eeyore's ears, eyes and eyebrows usually droop downward.

Step 5

Erase the construction lines and clean up the drawing.

Step 6

Colour your picture of Eeyore!

The Story of

Hi! My name is Marlin – you know, Nemo's father. I'm here to tell you a story. It's all about finding my son . . . finding Nemo. Years ago, Coral, my dear wife, and I were watching over our hundreds of eggs in our new home at the Drop-off. Suddenly a barracuda attacked, and Coral and all the eggs were taken from me. I was devastated.

Then I saw one tiny damaged egg left. I named the newborn Nemo and promised I would never let anything happen to him.

Nemo is a great little guy, despite the fact that when he was younger he was much too curious and adventurous for an overprotective father like me. He was born with one damaged fin, which I called his "lucky" fin. Unfortunately this lucky fin kept him from being a great swimmer. And that made me worry even more.

I kept Nemo out of school for as long as I could, but I finally had to give in. After all, I couldn't send a teenager off to first grade! On the first day of school, I thought I would be okay until I learned that their first field trip was going to the dangerous Drop-off! I raced after the class and found Nemo at the edge of the deep water!

I admit I panicked. I embarrassed poor Nemo so much that he felt he had to prove he was brave and strong. Before I knew it, he was swimming out to the deep water. He tagged a boat, impressing his new school friends. But then something terrible happened: A scuba diver swam up behind my son and netted him!

I raced off to find Nemo but couldn't keep up with the boat. That's where Dory came in. She's this silly and friendly blue tang who can't remember a thing! Still, she wanted to help, and I was grateful. She even came up with our first clue. You see, Dory read the address on the diver's mask that ended up on the ocean floor. It said: P. Sherman, 42 Wallaby Way, Sydney.

Meanwhile Nemo was stuck in a fish tank in P. Sherman's dental office in Sydney. Nemo made friends with a group of goofy fish, and when they learned that the dentist was going to give Nemo to his niece Darla, they quickly set up a plan to save him. You see, Darla was bad news for fish. She liked to shake them to death!

The tank's leader, Gill, thought up a plan for the tank fish to escape to the ocean. They were going to make the tank as dirty as possible so the dentist would have to clean it. That meant taking the fish out of the tank and putting them in plastic bags on the counter. From there, they would hop in their bags over to the window and jump into the harbour. (Why didn't they just serve themselves up on skewers and leap onto the barbecue? And they call *me* a "clownfish!")

Anyway Gill took Nemo under his fin to help him become a stronger swimmer. But their plan was foiled when the dentist installed a brand-new filter that was guaranteed to keep the tank clean . . . no matter how hard the fish tried to make it dirty.

85

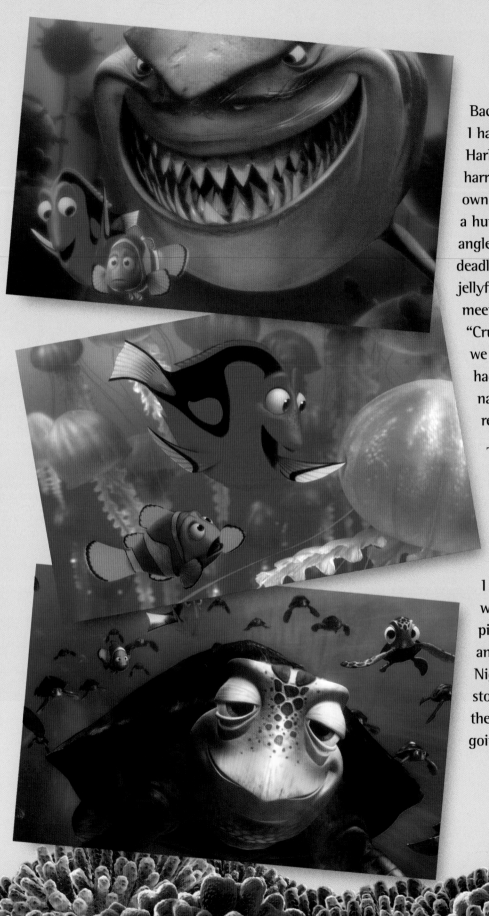

Back in the ocean, Dory and I had finally reached Sydney Harbour after some pretty harrowing adventures of our own – including run-ins with a hungry shark, a vicious anglerfish, and an almost-deadly forest of stinging jellyfish. The best part was meeting this cool turtle named "Crush" who rescued us after we escaped the jellyfish. He had the cutest little son named "Squirt" who reminded me of Nemo.

Then, when we got to the harbour, a pelican tried to eat us for breakfast! But I figured I had travelled so far to find Nemo that I wasn't about to give up. I fought like crazy. We were coughed up and picked up off the dock by another pelican named Nigel. Somehow he knew my story and took us right to the dentist's office. I was going to find my son!

Little did we know that Darla had arrived, ready for her present. The dentist scooped Nemo into a little plastic bag. But Nemo tricked the guy by playing dead. The tank fish realized Nemo was trying the "toilet escape" – he would get flushed down the toilet and make his way to the ocean. The fish were ecstatic . . . until the dentist headed for the trash can!

When Dory, Nigel, and I got there, I saw Nemo, looking dead as could be, floating in that little plastic bag. I was overcome with grief. I had no idea the little guy was actually still alive! The dentist pushed Nigel out the window, and the friendly pelican took Dory and me back to the harbour.

Meanwhile the tank fish launched Gill out of the tank to save Nemo. He hit a dental mirror that Nemo was resting on and sent Nemo flying into the spit sink and down the drain into the harbour!

Minutes later Dory ran into Nemo in the harbour. I had already left Dory because I was so sad that I wanted to be alone. It took her a little while to recognize Nemo, but when she did, they raced off together until they found me! But then a huge fishing net came down and trapped a bunch of fish, including Dory! Nemo got an idea. If the fish "swam down," they could pull on the net and break free. Nemo wanted to get into the net with the doomed fish to help them! I was beside myself – I had finally found my son, and now he wanted to risk his life! Well I finally let him go, and it worked! The fish were freed, and Nemo and I shared a really happy reunion. Dory joined right in.

When Dory, Nemo, and I made our way home to the reef, Nemo was excited about going back to school. And this time, I was ready to let him go.

Oh, and last I heard, Nemo's tank friends were floating in little plastic bags in the harbour. Seems Gill's escape plan finally worked . . .

N e m o

Clownfish

You remember Nemo. He's my son – the adventurous little fish with the "lucky" fin who longs for excitement and friends to play with. But instead, he's saddled with me, an overprotective single dad who never lets the poor little guy out of sight.

Well, one day, Nemo dares to show his friends he's not scared of the ocean (the way his dad is), and he swims off alone. He ends up getting a lot more excitement than he bargained for! But he also discovers just how brave and resourceful he can be. That's my boy!

from side, Nemo is shaped like Goldfish® cracker

from front, body looks like gumdrop

1

2

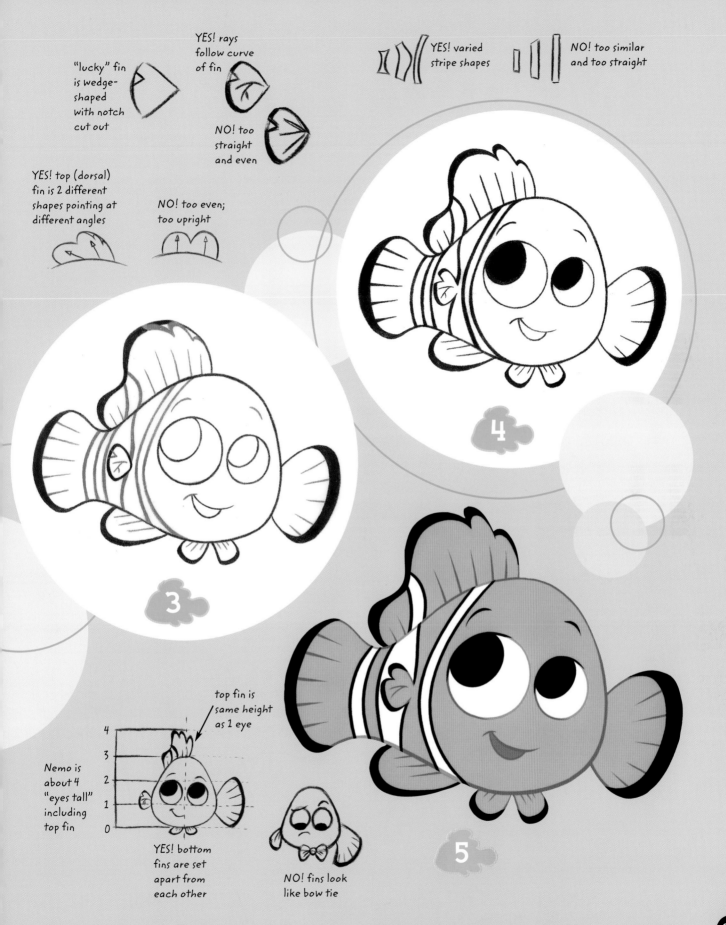

"lucky" fin is wedge-shaped with notch cut out

YES! rays follow curve of fin

NO! too straight and even

YES! varied stripe shapes

NO! too similar and too straight

YES! top (dorsal) fin is 2 different shapes pointing at different angles

NO! too even; too upright

Nemo is about 4 "eyes tall" including top fin

top fin is same height as 1 eye

4
3
2
1
0

YES! bottom fins are set apart from each other

NO! fins look like bow tie

3

4

5

Marlin

Clownfish

I'm that not-so-funny clownfish, Marlin (Nemo's dad). After losing almost all my family, I sort of become crazy about doing everything possible to keep my only son safe from the dangerous ocean. Unfortunately I go a little overboard and don't allow Nemo to do anything – I don't even let him go to school!

I fuss and fret a lot, but I really do mean well. It takes a little journey across the ocean, and meeting up with Dory, to teach me the meaning of trust and letting go. When it comes down to it, I'm just a regular dad who will do anything for his son.

1

Marlin is about 2 times the size of Nemo

2

rays on Marlin's fins and tail radiate out from "meaty" parts of body like this . . .

"meaty" parts

. . . not like this

face is kind of flat

5 rays on side (pectoral) fins and tail

from side, shaped like turkey drumstick

bags under eyes make him look tired

YES! eyes close together

NO! eyes too far apart

3

4

5

Dory

Regal Blue Tang

Dory is one chatty, friendly, funny fish! She never gives up hope – when things get tough, she just keeps on swimming. Always willing and helpful, Dory has everything going for her except for one small thing – her memory. She can't remember anything! But she risks her own life to help me find Nemo (despite the fact that she can't remember the little guy's name!).

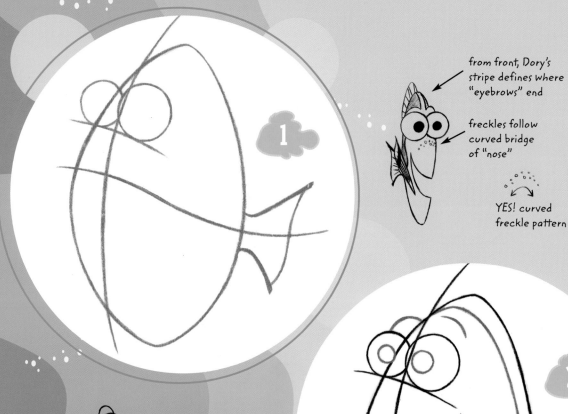

from front, Dory's stripe defines where "eyebrows" end

freckles follow curved bridge of "nose"

YES! curved freckle pattern

NO! too straight

Dory is just over 4 times the size of Nemo

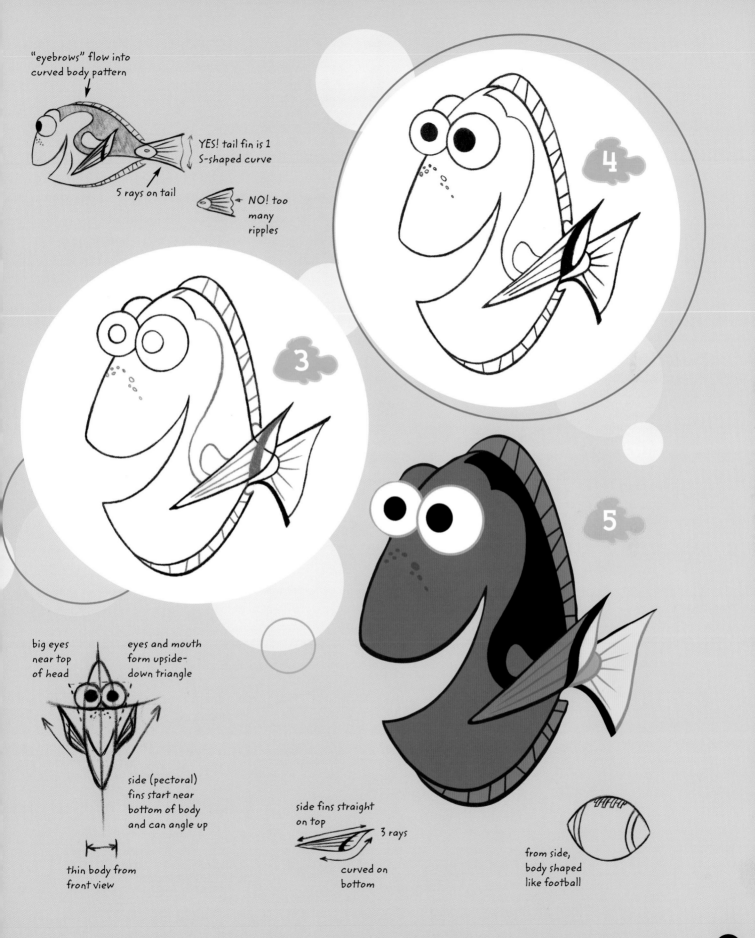

"eyebrows" flow into
curved body pattern

YES! tail fin is 1
S-shaped curve

5 rays on tail

NO! too
many
ripples

4

3

5

big eyes
near top
of head

eyes and mouth
form upside-
down triangle

side (pectoral)
fins start near
bottom of body
and can angle up

thin body from
front view

side fins straight
on top

3 rays

curved on
bottom

from side,
body shaped
like football

Gill

Moorish Idol

Gill is the leader of the tank fish – a group of fish trapped in a tank in a dentist's office. According to Nemo, Gill is charming, likable, tough and determined to break his friends out of the tank. He takes Nemo under his "scarred" fin to teach him the ropes and gives Nemo a part to play in the great escape he's been planning for years. Gill is a dreamer, a believer, and a doer, and I'll always be grateful to him.

YES! big, blocky eyebrows

NO! brows are too thin

eyes usually half closed

one line under each eye

Gill is about 14 times the size of Nemo

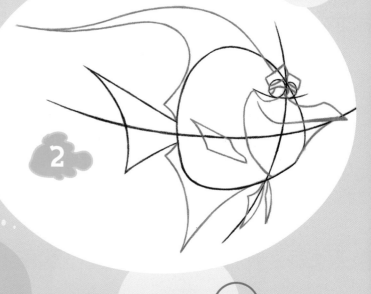

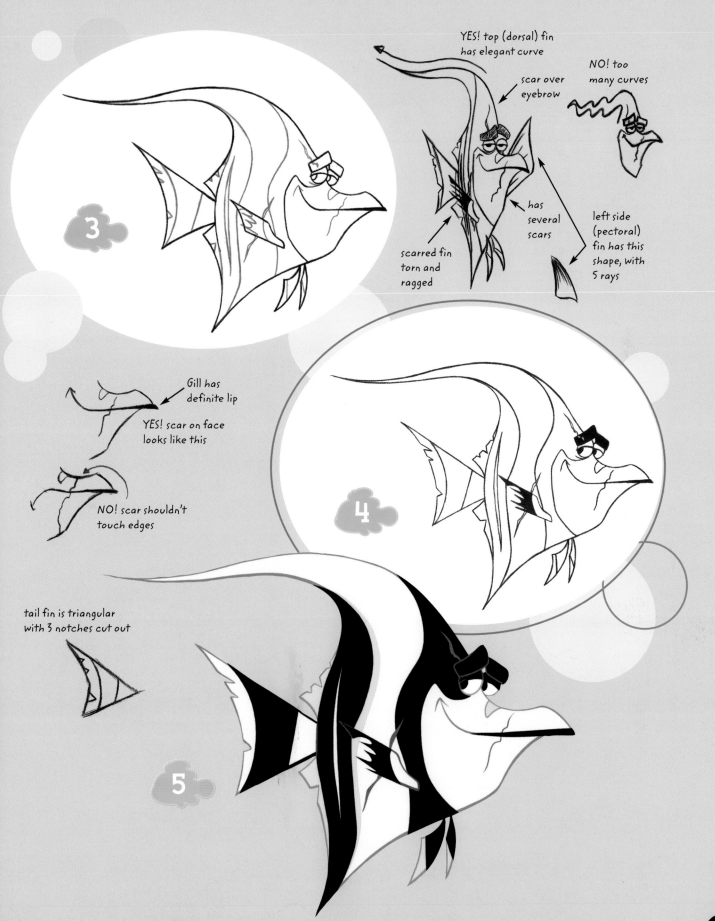

YES! top (dorsal) fin has elegant curve

scar over eyebrow

NO! too many curves

has several scars

scarred fin torn and ragged

left side (pectoral) fin has this shape, with 5 rays

Gill has definite lip

YES! scar on face looks like this

NO! scar shouldn't touch edges

tail fin is triangular with 3 notches cut out

3

4

5

Bloat

Blowfish

Bloat is a blowfish who holds it together until he can't take it anymore. Then he literally blows up like a balloon. He is Gill's trusted lieutenant in running the tank business. However, the stress of living in the tank often gets to him. Poor guy!

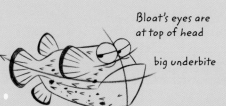

Bloat's eyes are at top of head

big underbite

YES! when Bloat isn't puffed out, "spikes" follow action of body and point toward tail

NO! spikes too upright

Bloat is about 4 times the size of Nemo (when he's not puffed out or "bloated")

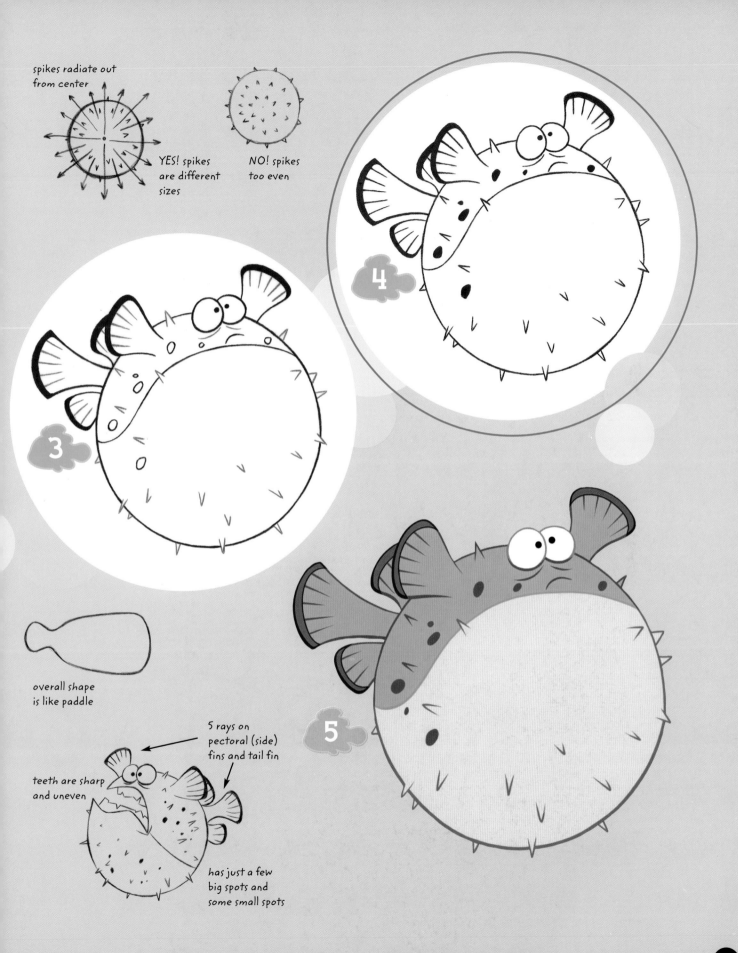

spikes radiate out
from center

YES! spikes
are different
sizes

NO! spikes
too even

3

4

overall shape
is like paddle

5 rays on
pectoral (side)
fins and tail fin

teeth are sharp
and uneven

has just a few
big spots and
some small spots

5

Bubbles

Yellow Tang

Did you ever hear the saying, "life is just a bowl of bubbles?" Well for Bubbles, it is. This crazy fish is in love with bubbles. He faithfully waits for bubbles to burst from the tank's plastic treasure chest and then joyously scrambles to put them back in. He never tires of this game, and he keeps the other fish amused. For Bubbles, it's all about the bubbles.

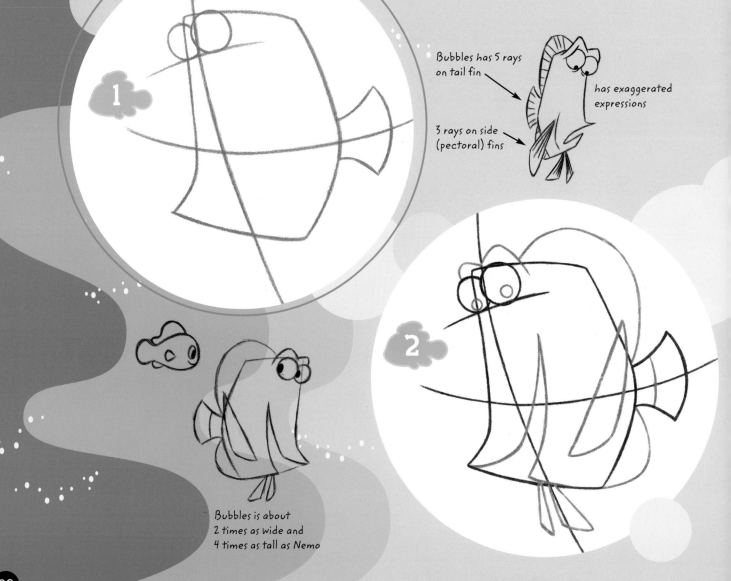

Bubbles has 5 rays on tail fin

has exaggerated expressions

3 rays on side (pectoral) fins

Bubbles is about 2 times as wide and 4 times as tall as Nemo

eyes sit right at top of head

eyebrows are expressive

3

4

5

eyelids add expression too

smile pushes cheek up to overlap eye slightly

side fins are like arms— used to collect bubbles

YES! just slightly angular top (dorsal) fin

NO! shape too smooth

top lip comes to point

YES! rays on top fin are irregular

NO! rays too evenly spaced and aligned

D e b (and Flo)

Black-and-White Humbug

Next we have Deb and her twin sister, Flo. The two of them are inseparable. They go everywhere and do everything together. They joke, swim and tell secrets – but only to each other. They look and act exactly alike. In fact, they are so much alike that one would think they were one and the same fish – which they are. Are you following this? You see, the tank fish don't have the heart to tell Deb that Flo is her reflection in the tank glass.

Deb talks to her own reflection

Deb is about 2 times the size of Nemo

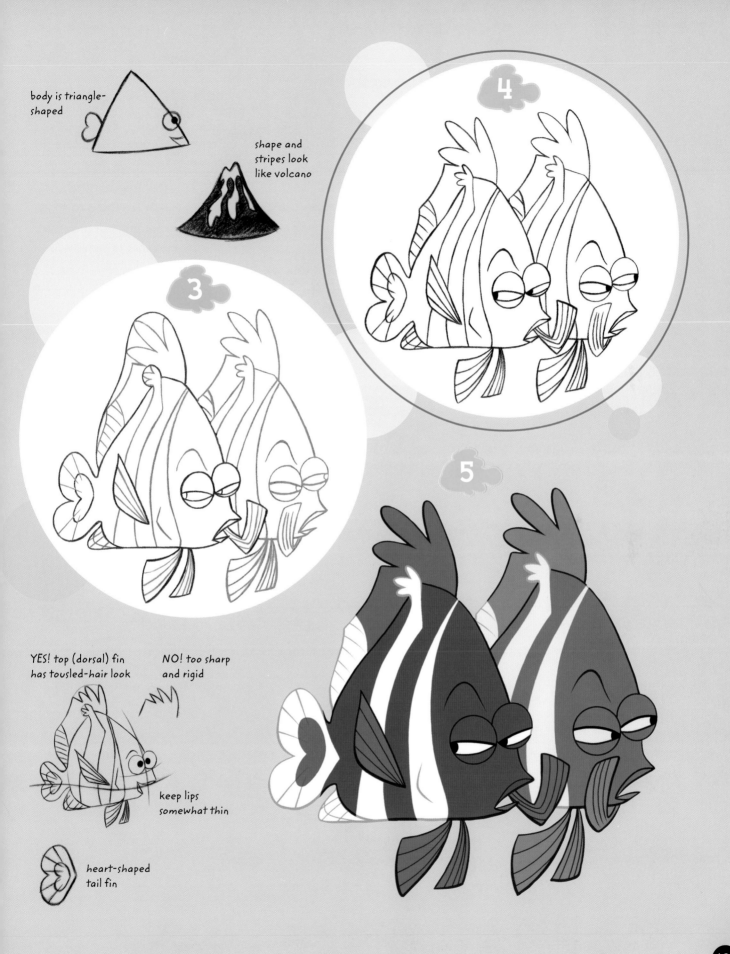

body is triangle-shaped

shape and stripes look like volcano

3

4

5

YES! top (dorsal) fin has tousled-hair look

NO! too sharp and rigid

keep lips somewhat thin

heart-shaped tail fin

Gurgle

Royal Gramma

Here's a guy after my own heart. His name is Gurgle. Gurgle is a fussy little fish who refuses to touch anything around him. He's so afraid of germs that he is completely obsessed with them. He believes that if he steers clear of everything and everyone in the tank, his odds are better for a longer, happier life. How smart is that! Everybody knows that tank fish don't live forever, and Gurgle isn't taking any chances!

Gurgle's body curves like an oblong water balloon

Gurgle is about 2 times the size of Nemo

eyes sit on top of head

YES! lips
are angular

NO! lips
too rounded

YES! rounded
tail fin

NO! tail fin
too pointed

if flat, pattern
would look
like this . . .

. . . but on body,
pattern curves
as if wrapped
around tube

YES! pupils are oval

NO! pupils too round

pupils get smaller
when he's scared

Peach

Starfish

Meet Peach – the tank's star reporter. She spends day after day stuck up high on the glass wall of that tank. And what else is there to do but report back on everything she sees? Unfortunately life can be pretty boring in a dentist's office, except when the dentist is working on a patient. Peach has watched countless hours of dental procedures, so she is the tank's dental expert. She spends the rest of her days counting floor tiles and watching the plants die.

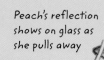

Peach's reflection shows on glass as she pulls away

Peach is about 3 times the size of Nemo

YES! angles and
points are rounded

NO! too sharp

3

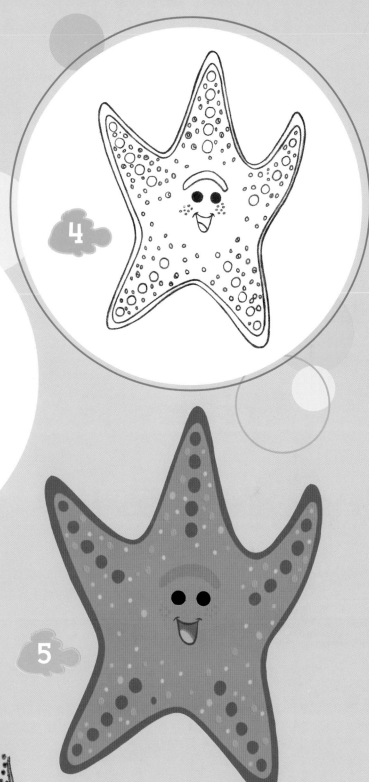

4

5

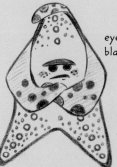

star points
work like
arms and legs

eyes are solid
black circles

YES! small spots are
various sizes and in
uneven pattern

5 main circles for
suction on each
arm (inside)

NO! spots
too even

eyebrows and
shape of eyes show
her expression

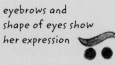

Jacques

Cleaner Shrimp

Jacques is a true original. He is one shrimp who loves to clean. He would clean the tank from morning until night if he could. I can see where cleaning could help a fish relax a little. After all, I like a nice clean reef myself! Jacques is like a good soldier: he's a born fighter, always doing battle with his greatest enemy – tank scum.

Jacques' facial feelers resemble a moustache

Jacques is just half the size of Nemo

YES! eyes overlap

NO! too far apart

legs spiky and notched

"hands" are like mitts

3

4

tail fin has 1 large spot and 2 small ones

YES! thin dark stripes

NO! dark stripes too thick

body always curves

5

Sharks

Now even I have a hard time with these fellows. Meet Bruce, Anchor, and Chum – three good friends who are inseparable. Anchor is the moody one who hates dolphins. Chum is always on the go; he just can't keep still. And Bruce is the happy-go-lucky leader of the pack. These sharks want to be friends with everyone under the sea. The only problem is, when we other fish see them coming, we all go swimming! Who knew they'd given up eating us? They've even formed a support group, and they have meetings to help promote their vegetarian lifestyle. Good luck, fellas!

Chum – Mako
Anchor – Hammerhead
Bruce – Great White

1

Chum

2

3

Chum's overall shape is like long, sharp knife

YES! angled eye shape

NO! eye too straight and square

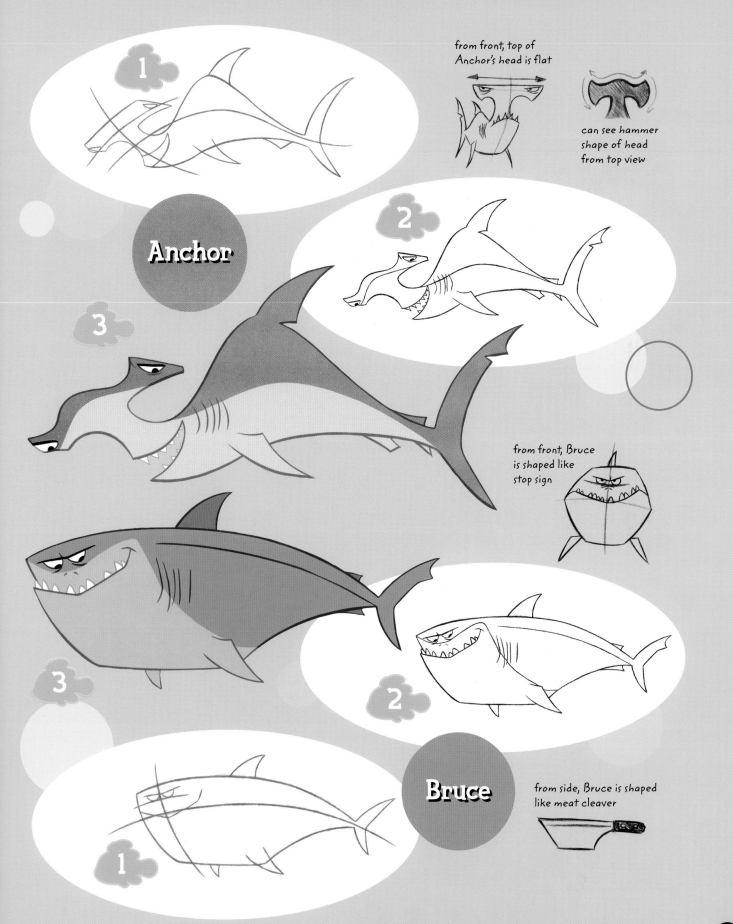

from front, top of
Anchor's head is flat

can see hammer
shape of head
from top view

Anchor

from front, Bruce
is shaped like
stop sign

Bruce

from side, Bruce is shaped
like meat cleaver

THE MAKING OF

Disney · PIXAR TOY STORY

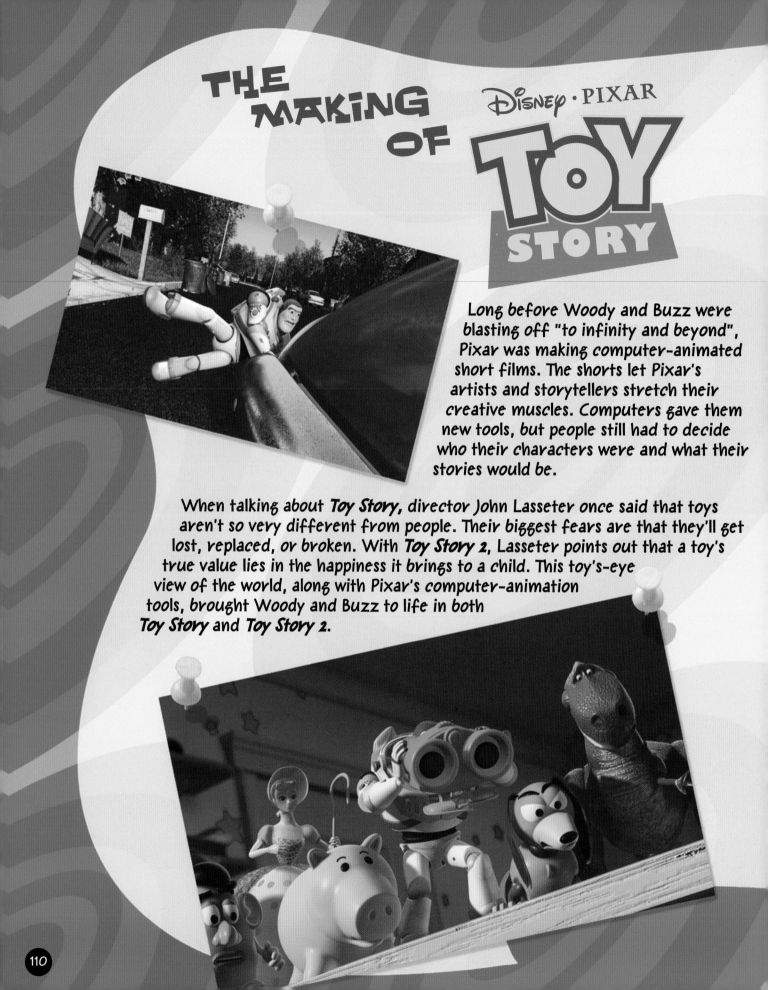

Long before Woody and Buzz were blasting off "to infinity and beyond", Pixar was making computer-animated short films. The shorts let Pixar's artists and storytellers stretch their creative muscles. Computers gave them new tools, but people still had to decide who their characters were and what their stories would be.

When talking about *Toy Story*, director John Lasseter once said that toys aren't so very different from people. Their biggest fears are that they'll get lost, replaced, or broken. With *Toy Story 2*, Lasseter points out that a toy's true value lies in the happiness it brings to a child. This toy's-eye view of the world, along with Pixar's computer-animation tools, brought Woody and Buzz to life in both *Toy Story* and *Toy Story 2*.

When Pixar and Walt Disney Feature Animation first teamed up, they developed the Computer Animated Production System – CAPS for short. This system let animators draw and paint an image using computers instead of brushes. The teamwork between Pixar and Disney led to **Toy Story**, the first full-length computer-animated feature film (and Academy Award winner!).

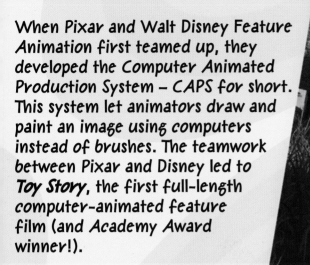

The fun of both **Toy Story** and **Toy Story 2** is that they let you see what happens after people "leave the room". When humans are present, the toys hold still and have only one expression. Once they are alone, however, the toys come to life. Their actions and their expressions show that they have just as many feelings as do the people in their world.

As you step into the toys' world, remember: A toy is not a toy until someone plays with it. So play with your drawings – have fun with the poses, expressions, and environments! Think like a toy . . . feel like a toy . . . and you'll bring your own "toy story" to life.

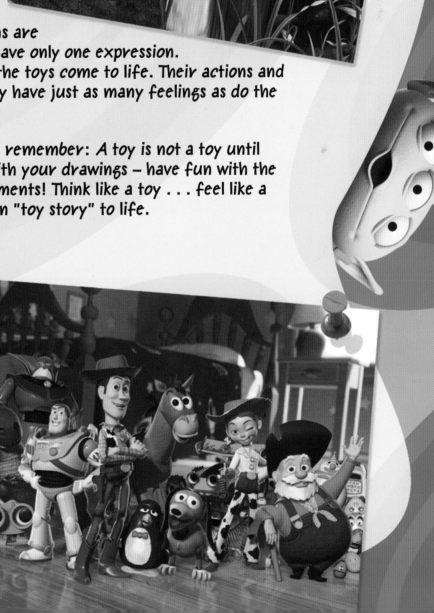

CHARACTER LINEUP

Before you begin drawing, check out the size relationships among the different characters, and look at their body proportions. How long is Slinky Dog compared to his height? How much taller than Hamm is Bullseye?

Bullseye

Prospector

Artists often use head size as a unit of measurement; for example, Buzz is about 4½ heads tall.

SPACE RANGER LIGHTYEAR

Hamm

Bo Peep

Zurg

Buzz Lightyear

Woody

Jessie

Notice that Woody is almost a head taller than Buzz, although Buzz's wingspan makes him much wider!

Tough and mighty, the Green Army Men are the smallest toys in the bunch, reaching only as high as the Alien's armpit.

Slinky Dog

Green Army Man

Alien

Rex

Rex may seem huge and imposing, but as you can see, he's barely taller than Bo Peep!

WOODY

top half of head (down to the bottom of nose) is a circle

STEP 1

Woody is top toy in both *Toy Story* and *Toy Story 2*. That's a tough spot to share, especially with a new toy named Buzz Lightyear, who thinks he's a space ranger. But Woody takes it all in his stride. After all, he's one tough cowboy. And he's smart enough to know that the best part about being a toy is having a special kid like Andy to play with.

nose is a little below halfway between top of head and jaw

STEP 2

round eyes are above halfway point between top of head and jaw

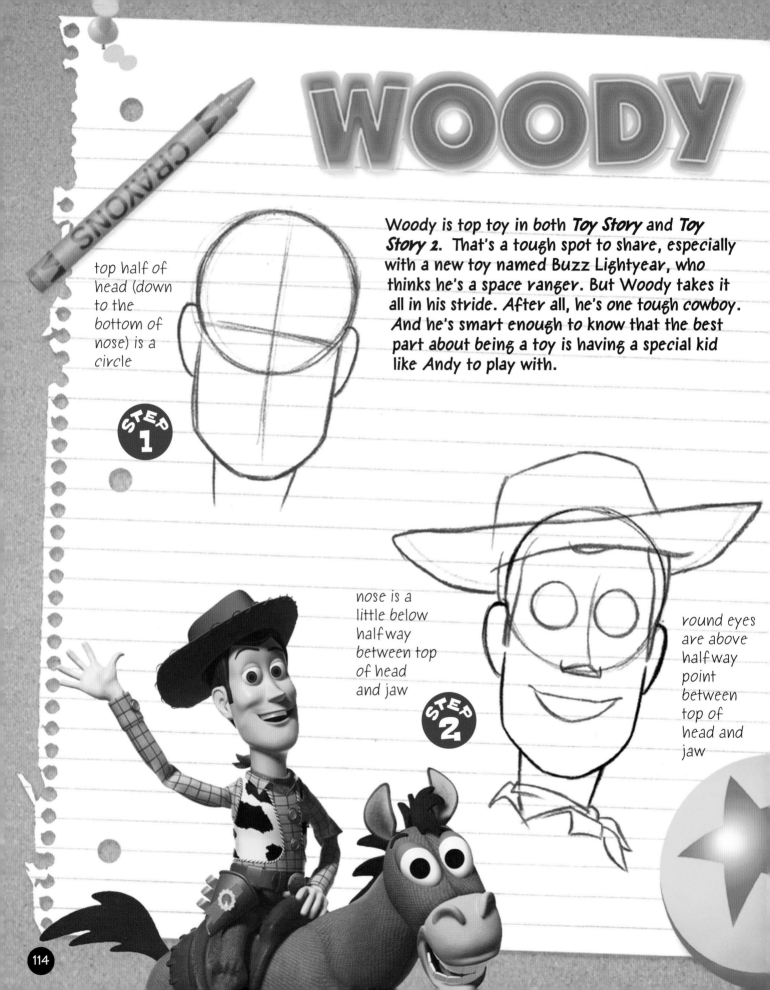

114

hair curl is like the letter "C"

STEP 3

round eyes

large iris (1/2 of eye)

bottom half of head shows off Woody's square jawline

too straight

NO!

NO!

YES!

show nostril side on 3/4 view or profile

ears are flat on top

teeth are one long rectangle

YES!

STEP 4

NO!

115

WOODY

top view of Woody's hat

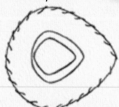

triangular with stitching around the edges

hat cross-section; hat band comes up 1/4 of hat height

8-pointed spurs

Sheriff Woody was once the star of Woody's Roundup, a popular 1950's TV show for kids. On the show, Woody was actually a marionette, but his accessories made him one nifty toy.

buckle has steer-head design

hat fits squarely on head

bandanna accents silhouette

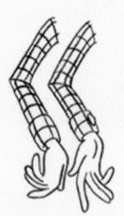

sleeve buttons on inside of elbow

sheriff's badge is a 5-point star

ears are wedge-shaped

arms and legs are made up of tubular sections that are pinched at the knees and elbows

forearms are longer than upper arms

calves are longer than thighs

Woody is about as tall as 4 of his own heads

STEP 1

STEP 2

STEP 3

STEP 4

CRAYONS

Colour Palette

torso is bean-shaped;
head and torso are
the same height

117

BULLSEYE

Bullseye, the sharpest horse in the West, is a trusty, energetic pony that loves Woody more than anything else in the world. This proud pony would do almost anything to keep his favourite sheriff out of harm's way.

legs are loose and floppy

YES! eyes slant apart slightly

head is shaped roughly like a capsule

ears roll like felt

NO! too much slant

STEP 2

STEP 1

3 locks go forward

4½ locks go down like a saw blade

mouth low on muzzle

legs consist of two
individually stuffed
sections – almost
shaped like peanuts

try to keep
a clear line
of action

bottom of hoof
shows hollowed-
out centre

bottom points
of tail line up

CRAYONS

STEP
4

STEP
3

Colour
Palette

119

Jessie

Jessie knows what it means to be a toy. She once belonged to a little girl who loved her as much as Andy loves Woody. But that little girl gave Jessie away, and the broken-hearted toy decided that being a collectible is better than being with a child who might outgrow you. Woody has to remind Jessie what being a toy is all about — and convince her to come back to Andy's room with him.

rag-doll body is flexible

she has a button nose

YES!

NO! too big

5 pieces of fringe attach to outside edge of chaps

chaps wrap around front of jeans

chaps looser on bottom to allow for boots

pull string on back

hat usually sits on the back of her head

torso is shaped like a peanut

shirt and gauntlet pattern

stitching wraps around cuff

3 fringe pieces

Woody's hat
is triangular

Jessie's hat
is rounder

STEP 1

ponytail
hangs
down
back

STEP 2

STEP 3

Colour
Palette

STEP 4

THE PROSPECTOR

The Prospector may seem like a nice grand-fatherly type of fellow at first, but when his true feelings are revealed, it becomes clear that he's just plain selfish and mean. Having never belonged to a child, the Prospector simply doesn't know how to play – or be loved.

STEP 1

legs are small in proportion to rest of body

head shaped like a bell

moustache reacts to moods

beard, brows, and moustache are loose and bushy

quick gesture drawings can help show emotion

relaxed gesture

STEP 2

stretch

excited gesture

body like a half-filled flour sack

squash

CRAYONS

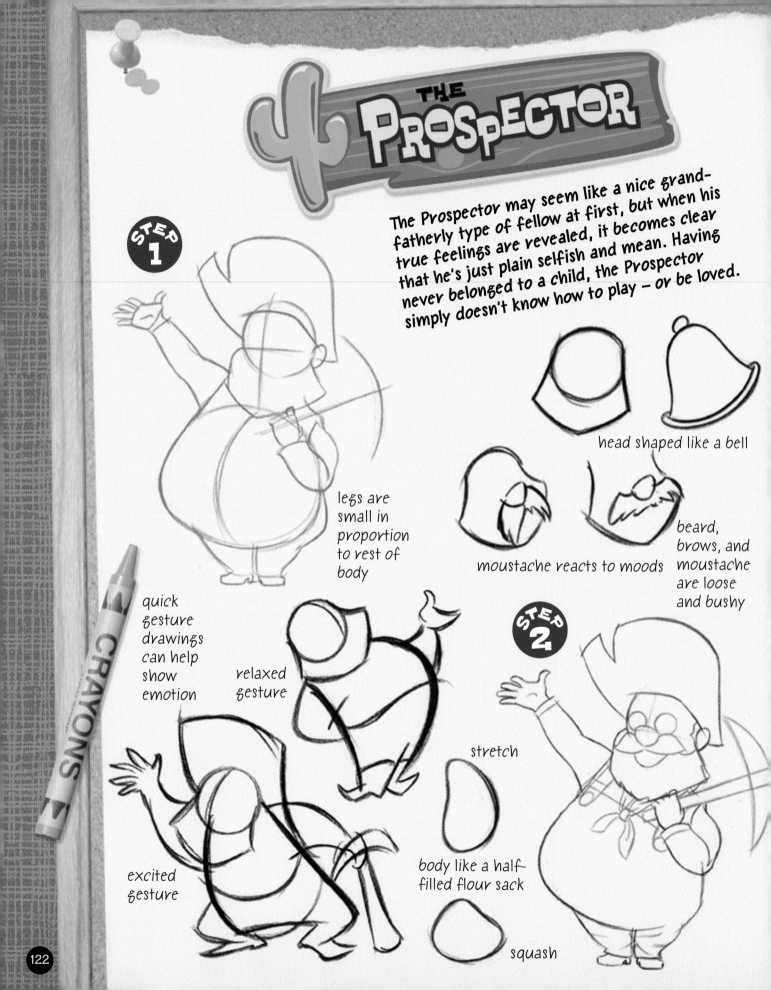

CRAYONS

STEP 3

arms taper
at wrist

Prospector is
never without
his pickaxe

boot flares
at top

hat curls up in
front and back

STEP 4

pointy
beard in side
view

small hands with
rather slender
fingers

tight-fitting
sleeves

button
detail

Colour Palette

123

Buzz Lightyear

Buzz has stars in his eyes until Woody pulls him back down to earth. For most of *Toy Story*, Buzz doesn't understand that he's a toy. But in *Toy Story 2*, he understands so well that he has to remind Woody.

STEP 1

STEP 2

basic head shape rectangular; jaw drawn into bottom half of a hexagon

chin cleft looks like number "9"

Buzz's chin takes up about 1/3 of his head

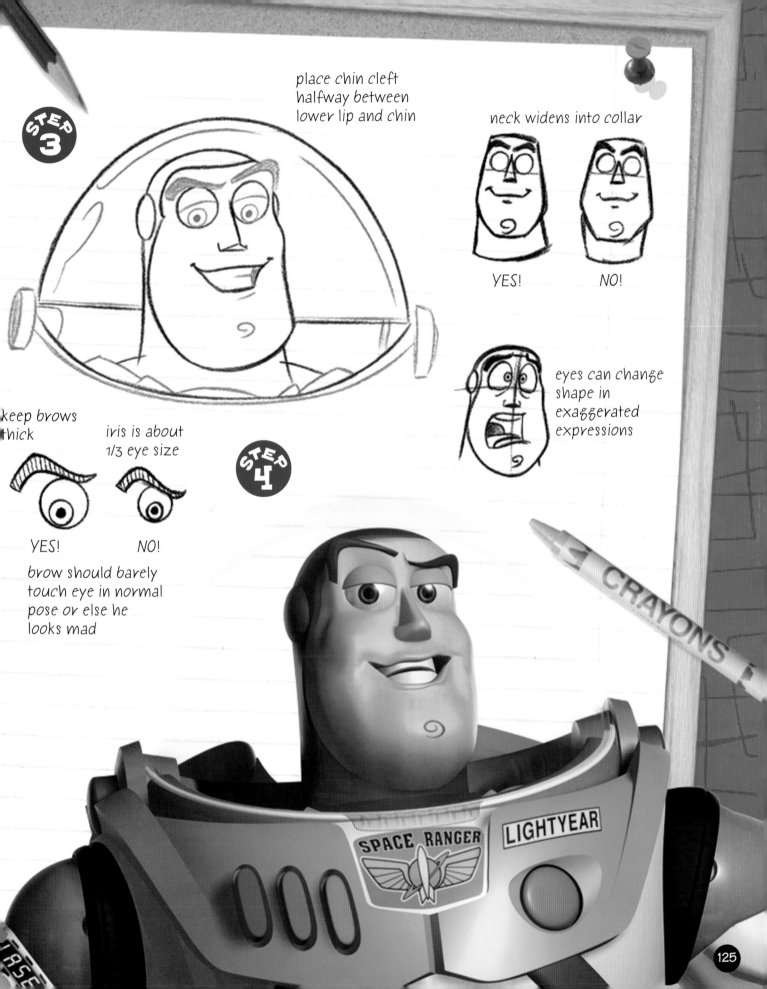

STEP 3

place chin cleft halfway between lower lip and chin

neck widens into collar

YES!   NO!

eyes can change shape in exaggerated expressions

keep brows thick

iris is about 1/3 eye size

STEP 4

YES!   NO!

brow should barely touch eye in normal pose or else he looks mad

CRAYONS

SPACE RANGER   LIGHTYEAR

When Buzz first comes to Andy's room, the other toys are in awe of his cool accessories. But Buzz learns a lesson in humility in **Toy Story 2** when he is confronted by a newer, shinier version of Buzz Lightyear.

STEP 1

STEP 2

4 grooves on shoe sole

legs consist of two sections connected by ball joints

fingers are tubular

angled

straight

full wingspan is about 3 shoulder widths

arms consist of cylinders and spheres

basic shape of backpack is like a turtle's shell

STEP 3

STEP 4

Colour Palette

SPACE RANGER LIGHTYEAR

127

ZURG

The universe – including Al's Toy Barn – is not a safe place with the evil Emperor Zurg on the loose. Zurg is smart enough to escape from the store and strong enough to take on Buzz and New Buzz – but unlucky enough to be on the receiving end of Rex's swinging tail.

hands are composed of sharp steel parts with clawlike fingers

fingers resemble armour plates

head composed of many triangular shapes

angle of horns is about 45 degrees

YES!

NO!

NO!

evil "Z" shape on cape clasp

5 torso rings

Zurg's gauntlet

Buzz's gauntlet

concave at top

convex at top

cape can flow for dramatic effect

"Feet" are three wheels

visor appears triangular in all views

8 glowing yellow teeth

STEP
1

STEP
2

STEP
3

STEP
4

Colour Palette

REX

This toy dinosaur is one nervous Rex. When he's not worried about being replaced by a bigger dino toy, he's trying to avoid conflict in Andy's room. Rex's growl "almost" scares the other toys.

STEP 1

tail tapers to a point

basic eye expression

pupils are tiny

"hmmm"

"what did I step in?"

"the sky is falling!"

STEP 2

mouth expressions

"yikes!"

"ooooh!"

Teeth are cone-shaped

"aahhh!"

upper body flows smoothly from spherical lower body

head is block-shaped

legs attach high on lower body

legs similar to a human's – only thicker

side of foot is wedge-shaped with rounded corners

toenails are diamond-shaped with a centre line

back of foot

note distance between toenails

tiny arms with clawed fingers

torso is pear-shaped

STEP 3

knee is just above belly

STEP 4

thick neck tapers to head

Colour Palette

CRAYONS

Bo Peep

When Bo Peep isn't minding her sheep, she's got her eye on Woody. Although "Bo" is part of baby Molly's lamp, she definitely is not a preschool toy. Bo Peep is wise, and she believes in Woody no matter what happens.

dress looks like a parasol

pantaloons look like tiers

STEP 1

STEP 2

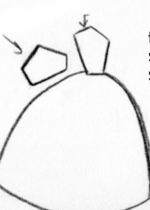

house shape

turn house on side to get basic shape of bust

basic wedge
shape of hat

add curves
and details

NO! neck
too short

CRAYONS

3 locks of
curls on back
of head

YES! neck is
long

eyes come
halfway
down head

mouth is
upside-down
triangle

STEP
3

nose is
wedge-
shaped

profile starts
with a circle

STEP
4

Colour Palette

133

HAMM

You can always count on Hamm to put in his two cents on any topic. As Andy's piggy bank and Mr. Potato Head's buddy (spuddy?), Hamm says what he thinks . . . especially when he thinks Woody's headed for trouble.

STEP 1

STEP 2

Colour Palette

don't forget his tail and cork!

pear-shaped body

small ears

three toes

- eyes high on head
- nostrils lie on top of halfway line on nose
- small bottom teeth

coin slot on
top of back

nose fits on
head like a
cup on a
sphere

mouth is a
small slit
on bottom
of snout

STEP 3

eyes squash
and stretch,
depending on
expression

STEP 4

SLINKY

"Slink" always has a spring in his step. He's a happy-go-lucky toy dog and one of Woody's strongest supporters in Andy's room. When Woody needs help in *Toy Story*, Slinky Dog goes the extra mile – or at least as far as his spring will stretch.

STEP 1

head is a ball

thick, heavy brows

very round eyes

STEP 2

body is 2 halves of sphere attached with a spring

eye lies halfway up on head circle

spring compresses and shortens body

STEP 3

back legs have bendable knees

Colour Palette

Slinky Dog is a pull toy, so he has a wheel on each foot.

STEP 4

Aliens

It's a very small world for the Alien toys at Pizza Planet. They live to see whom the claw will choose to leave their crane-game world.

While trapped inside the crane game, the Aliens obey the claw's calling, but when they escape, they are quick to find others to worship – like Mr. Potato Head, much to his chagrin.

STEP 1

STEP 2

STEP 3

Colour Palette

STEP 4

Green Army Men

STEP 2

STEP 3

Colour
Palette

STEP 4

Led by Sergeant, these soldiers are always ready for a Code Red. Whether they're parachuting from the second floor or running from a toy ball, the Green Army Men move with military precision. They don't miss a step when they march, even though their feet are attached to solid bases.

CRAYONS

139

Mutant Toys

What happens when Andy's toy-destroying next-door neighbour gets hold of a few good toys? He creates mutant toys – a baby-faced doll attached to spider legs, a ducky attached to a launching spring, and a frog on wheels. But when push comes to shove, these toys prove to be as loyal and friendly as any of the intact toys from Andy's room.

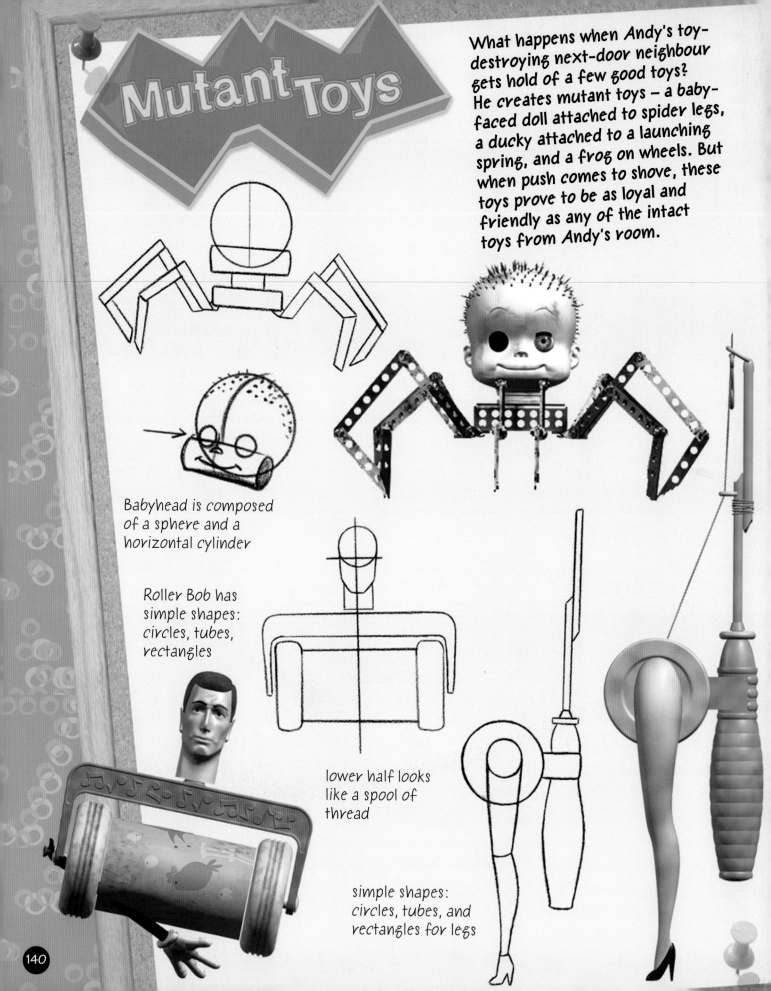

Babyhead is composed of a sphere and a horizontal cylinder

Roller Bob has simple shapes: circles, tubes, rectangles

lower half looks like a spool of thread

simple shapes: circles, tubes, and rectangles for legs

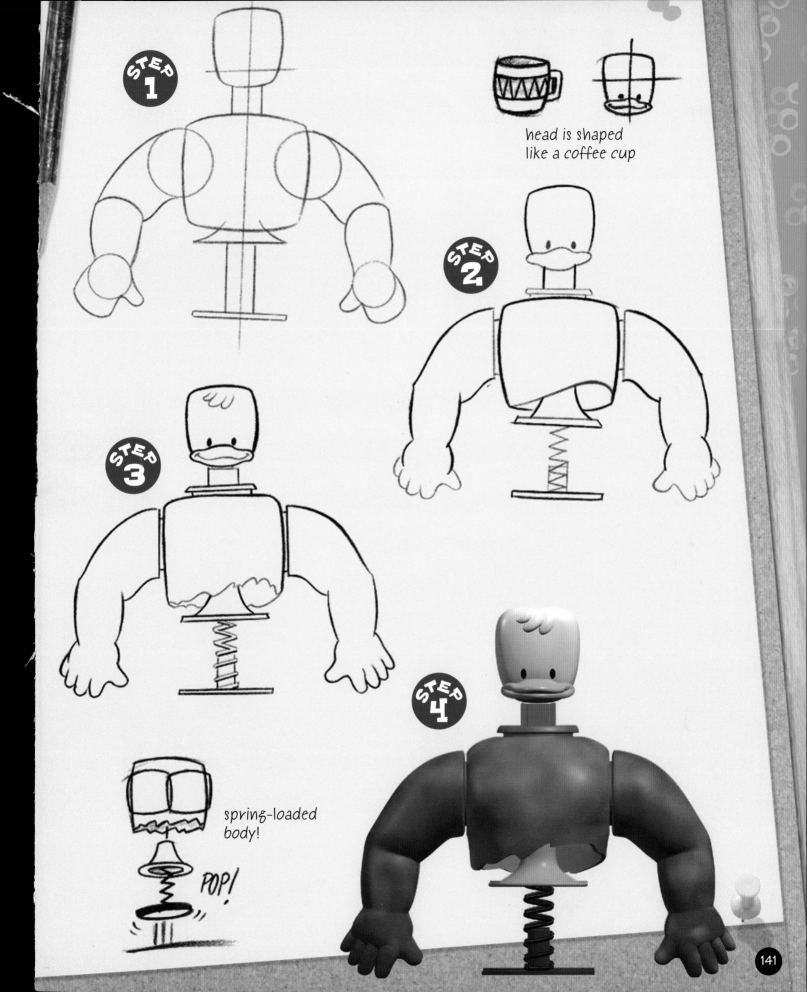

STEP 1

STEP 2

head is shaped
like a coffee cup

STEP 3

STEP 4

spring-loaded
body!

POP!